DISCOVER T[...]
TRUTHS ABOU[...]
AND WHO YOU WERE

Past life regression can reveal:

- The traumas buried in your unconscious—perhaps from centuries ago
- The source of physical pain that seems to have no cause
- The real reason so many people claim they were Judas, an Egyptian princess, Mark Twain, or other famous characters in a past life—and what their belief really means
- The spirit guide waiting to help you explore your past . . . and your future
- The soul, what it is, its eternal form, and its purpose in this world . . . and the next
- Your present body—why you chose it and what your mission in this lifetime may be
- And much more—including author Brad Steiger's own past life experience and how recalling it instantly freed him from a phobia that had troubled him for years.

"Brad Steiger's unique combination of open curiosity and careful scholarship combine to make this book a very good read. . . . He provides the reader with a broad spectrum of ideas about the soul's journey toward enlightenment."
   —Rabbi Yonassan Gershom,
      author of *Beyond the Ashes:*
      Cases of Reincarnation from the Holocaust

"Brad Steiger has long been a true pioneer. . . . As you read [this book], let it trigger your own memories of who you have been throughout time and space."
                     —Bettye B. Binder, President of the
                        Association for Past-Life
                        Research and Therapies

"Of all the contemporary investigators of psychic phenomena and reincarnation, Brad Steiger was there first, inspiring us all. He . . . knows more about these subjects than anyone alive."
                     —Dick Sutphen, author of *You Were*
                        Born Again to be Together

RETURNING FROM THE LIGHT

Using Past Lives to Understand the Present and Shape the Future

Brad Steiger

A SIGNET BOOK

SIGNET
Published by the Penguin Group
Penguin Books USA Inc., 375 Hudson Street,
New York, New York 10014, U.S.A.
Penguin Books Ltd, 27 Wrights Lane,
London W8 5TZ, England
Penguin Books Australia Ltd, Ringwood,
Victoria, Australia
Penguin Books Canada Ltd, 10 Alcorn Avenue,
Toronto, Ontario, Canada M4V 3B2
Penguin Books (N.Z.) Ltd, 182–190 Wairau Road,
Auckland 10, New Zealand

Penguin Books Ltd, Registered Offices:
Harmondsworth, Middlesex, England

First published by Signet, an imprint of Dutton Signet,
a division of Penguin Books USA Inc.

First Printing, April, 1996
10 9 8 7 6 5 4 3 2 1

Contents

CHAPTER ONE

Returning From the Light to Greater Awareness

For the first thirty-six years of my life I was convinced that I would die in an airplane crash.

Because of a series of nightmares that began when I was a small child, I had a full-blown, stomach-wrenching, heart-thudding, cold-sweat-producing, brain-dizzying, unreasoning fear of flying, which severely hampered my professional life.

I used to drive the publicity departments of my publishers absolutely crazy, because I would refuse to fly on promotional tours for my books. They would be forced to arrange connections for me by means of commuter trains, buses, and automobiles.

Sometimes, after a particularly wretched travel experience, such as being stranded for hours in a commuter train without air-conditioning on a sweltering July afternoon, I would resolve to fly on my next promotional junket. But then as soon as I would approach an air terminal, the same old gut-wrenching, sweat-popping, fear of flying would force me to cancel the flight plans and seek a route to the next talk show by bus or train or rented car.

I think the dreams first began when I was around six years old. I got my own room then, and the paper Mom had chosen for the walls was covered with images of sailors, sailboats, buoys, and lifesavers. Not a single airplane, interestingly enough.

In the beginning, I had only the impression of being high in the air, swooping through the clouds—and then I was hurtling toward the ground, certain to be killed.

By the time I was ten or eleven, the frightening scenario had added a few images. I was in an open cockpit, looking down on a scenic checkerboard of fields, meadows, farmhouses, and small villages. Then, suddenly, I was catapulted out of the small plane and sent plummeting toward the ground.

Around that time, in 1946, my first cousin LaFay "Kiddie" Olson married Bob Croker, who had been a P–51 fighter pilot with the 339th Fighter Group in England. Bob was a bona fide

"Ace," who had flown a total of fifty-three combat missions over Germany. In addition to downing a number of conventional Nazi fighters, Bob had the distinction of shooting down one of Germany's first experimental jet airplanes. He had won the Distinguished Flying Cross, the Air Medal, the Eame Ribbon, and three Bronze Stars.

So how could I refuse him when he wanted to take me up in his modified single engine crop duster?

Especially when my six-year-old kid sister June accepted the invitation without a blink of the eye.

I would never call my sister a tomboy, because she always retained her basic femininity. She was just always ready to try new things, and I learned early in life that males had by no means acquired a monopoly on daring and courage.

Ever the gentleman, I told June that she could have the first ride.

While she was aloft with Bob, I prayed that she would descend screaming and teary-eyed, complaining so strenuously of the terrible ordeal that I could clearly and understandably beg off from subjecting myself to a similar trial by airplane.

When she jumped out, grinning from ear to ear, and shouting over the roar of the engine to tell me how much fun it was—and now it was my turn—I had no choice but to crawl grim-faced into the small plane.

Although Bob loved to joke and kid around, I

begged him not to loop the loop and fly upside down the way he said he was going to. Whether it was the plaintive whimper in my voice or the very real concern that I might vomit all over his cockpit, Bob delivered me back to terra firma before I had fainted. All I remember about the airplane ride was glimpsing the town's water tower from a very different perspective.

That night the awful dream came to me with added terrors. Now I was swooping high above the patchwork fields, feeling as though I were desperately trying to escape from something pursuing me. Suddenly, flames engulfed me. There was a blast of noise and fire—and then, once again, I was being hurtled toward the ground.

I was now old enough to attempt to understand my inner experiences and to interpret my dream. I decided that I was being shown a vision of my future: One day, I would die in an airplane crash after the vehicle had exploded in the air. I vowed that I would avoid air travel and thereby elude my fate.

In those days, avoiding flying was not really a problem. Automobiles sufficed to get me wherever I wanted to go.

But by 1967, I had written a number of successful books, and the various publishers' publicity people were now insisting that I make promotional trips to help sell my latest works.

There was no more escaping the problem. I had to try to come to grips with my fear of flying.

I was having absolutely no success with conquering my phobia until I had a profound past-life vision that completely eliminated my fear literally overnight.

Since that past-life recall I have logged several thousand miles of air travel each year. No anxiety attacks. No white knuckles. No tranquilizers.

The "cure" of my fear of flying cannot be attributed to years of psychoanalysis, encounter groups, or any in-vogue therapy. My decades' old phobia was conquered by the catharsis of my psyche having undergone my death experience in what appeared to be a vivid past-life memory.

I awakened one night early in 1972 to view, as if on an oversized television screen that had materialized on my bedroom wall, scenes from a city that appeared to have the flavor of Germany at the turn of the century. The moment I wondered about the year, I saw a calendar that told me that it was 1912.

I watched enthralled as I saw the details of a man's life unfolding before me. I seemed focused on a young attorney in Bremen, Germany, a man who found himself embroiled in great personal tragedy.

Then it came to me that I was perceiving the ensuing events *only through the eyes* of this one person, the young attorney. And interestingly, I could see this person *only* when he would pass in front of a mirror or some other reflective surface. Although his features were not the least bit similar to my own, I was somehow given to understand that this attorney in Bremen in the year 1912 was an expression of the same soul that manifests today as Brad Steiger.

Because of the turmoil that raged uncontrollably around him, the young attorney fled the city. He wandered throughout Europe for a number of years, studying, painting, writing. He seemed to be struggling with two opposing aspects of himself. One the one hand, he wished to elevate human consciousness through the expression of his art. On the other, he found himself becoming bitter and cynical at the growing materialism of his age.

At the outbreak of World War I, he returned to Germany and enlisted in the flying corps. From this point onward, he seemed only to live for the moment.

Then on an especially sunny afternoon, high in the skies over France, he and his squadron mates encountered a group of British aircraft. While he was diving after his chosen prey, he became aware of a stinging in his shoulder. He turned around to see blood spurting. A British aircraft with twin machine guns was right on his tail.

There was an explosion, a violent burst of

flame, and he was aware of falling unsupported through space.

It was at that point that I again became aware of the present-day reality around me. Sleep was now out of the question, but I recall that it probably took me an hour or so before I was centered enough to realize that I had just seen the events leading up to the nightmare scenario that had troubled me ever since I was a small boy. I had just seen the full scope of the awful dream that had placed me high in the air, engulfed me in a blast of noise and flame, and hurtled my body toward the ground.

Then it came to me in a rush of revelation: I was not fated to die in a midair explosion in my present life. I had *already died* in such an explosion in a previous life experience. Since earliest childhood, I had been troubled by the soul memory of a past life.

From that moment on, my fear of flying was eliminated; and the terrible nightmare of falling to my death was banished forever.

At the time of my past-life vision, I had already been actively researching reincarnation for about seven years. I have always been fascinated and challenged by the concept that we have lived before on this or other worlds or dimensions. One of my first published articles, "How Many People Are You?" (*Exploring the Unknown*, 1963) dealt with the subject of rebirth. My first book-length work on reincarnation was published in 1967 (*The Enigma of Reincarnation*).

Now I saw clearly that there was a practical side, a therapeutic, healing aspect to past-lives research. Oh, certainly, I had noticed on occasion a spontaneous alleviation of a subject's chronic condition while he or she was undergoing regression, but my principal interest in research at that time was to *prove* reincarnation.

But now it had happened to me! My long-term fear of flying had been cured because of one dramatic vision of witnessing my death in a former lifetime.

I remembered my present-life near-death experience as an eleven-year-old child. In my mind I saw once again the Light as I moved toward its brilliance, its peace, love, and tranquillity.

If we enter the Light and become One with it when we leave our physical bodies, then it might well be part of a natural process of spiritual evolution to return from the Light to complete lessons left unlearned, to finish work left undone.

Did an expression of my soul actually live in Germany at the turn of the century and die in aerial combat during World War I? Or had some creative facet of my psyche only fabricated a marvelously detailed psychodrama to provide me with a catharsis whereby I might now travel by air and achieve a much more effective schedule for conducting research, giving lectures, and fulfilling promotional activities?

Certainly there may be other explanations of my vision other than reincarnation. Maybe my psyche somehow attuned to the life pattern of someone who actually lived as an attorney in Bremen, Germany, prior to World War I; and I blended with his soul-memory long enough to make it seem as though I, myself, had those experiences in another lifetime.

Truly, from my perspective, it is not really important to me to gather data and documents to prove whether or not that German pilot who died in a fiery crash over the war-torn fields of France was truly a prior physical expression of my soul. I am very much aware that my present soul expression loathes war and that I have sought in my writings to help my brothers and sisters realize that they have the potential to transcend the primitive impulses that lead to inhumanity, bloodshed, and the desecration of the sacred bond that should unite all people in the Oneness of spirit.

Whatever the ultimate truth of my experience may be, the important thing is that the vision served a most useful and practical purpose. Because of that one mighty burst of creativity or past-life memory, a fear that had crippled me since childhood was removed.

And from the profound experience of that vision

onward, I began to perceive the knowledge of alleged past lives as a form of awareness.

In this present book, I will document some startling evidence—proof, if you will—of the reality of past-life experiences. But the prevailing theme of this work will be to illustrate how the awareness of past lives can help everyone to get it together in the present-life experience in order to begin to shape a more positive, productive, peaceful future.

Basically, the way past-lives therapy works is this: When subjects relive a past life during a regression or in a dream or in a vision, they become capable of accepting responsibility for a past action that was performed in that prior lifetime. Once the subjects have made the transfer of responsibility to the present life and have recognized that the "fault" lies in a time far removed from current concerns, they are able to deal with the matter without embarrassment or shame.

Throughout the pages of this book, you will meet numerous thoughtful and loving past-lives therapists who have learned that it really doesn't matter whether past-life recall is pure fantasy or the actual memory of a prior existence. What does matter is that thousands of men and women have obtained a definite and profound release from a present pain or phobia by reliving the origin of their problems in some real or imagined former existence.

CHAPTER TWO

Using Past-Life Memories to Solve Present-Life Problems

Richard Sutphen and I met in this life in 1977. By the time that we had completed a national tour of major U.S. cities, we had forged a firm and lasting friendship.

Dick began his hypnosis and past-lives regression work in 1972; and to the best of my knowledge, he was the first to develop a technique whereby one might regress large numbers of men and women to alleged former lifetimes, *en masse*.

Although every hypnotist he knew told him that there was no way to conduct group regressions, Dick started fine-tuning his style in his home with a roomful of people at a time. He continued perfecting his techniques in Phoenix-area colleges and high schools and at metaphysical gatherings in the Southwest.

In 1973, he founded and directed a hypnosis/metaphysical center in Scottsdale, Arizona. The convenience of working at an established center provided him with the structure that he needed to experiment extensively with both individual and group techniques and the opportunity to amass a large number of case histories for purposes of comparison and contrast.

In 1976, Dick created and marketed the first prerecorded hypnosis tapes through his Valley of the Sun publishing company. His inventory has grown to include 380 audio and video titles.

Dick's latest book, *Radical Spirituality* (Valley of the Sun, 1995) brings his total to eighteen volumes. He has appeared on hundreds of radio and television shows, and over 100,000 people have attended a Sutphen Seminar. A few years ago, Dick left the desert for the beach at Malibu, where he presently resides with his wife Tara and their children.

"Past-life hypnotic regression can be used as an extremely valuable therapeutic tool to explore the cause of unconscious anxiety, repressed hostilities, hidden fears, hangups, and interpersonal-relationship conflicts," Dick Sutphen said. "Past-life therapy is not a magic wand, and the past-life causes don't always surface immediately, but it does work; and it can be for many the first step in letting go of a problem.

"Psychiatrists often spend months or even years searching for the cause of their patient's problem. They are aware that in understanding the cause they can begin to mitigate and, eventually, eliminate the effect. Yet by limiting their search to the time frame of only one lifetime, they may never find the origin of the present-life problem."

Past-Life Regression Helped Barbara to Face Her Weight Problem

During one of his two-day past-life seminars, Dick Sutphen spoke with a woman named Barbara, who had driven hundreds of miles to be in attendance, because "someone up there" had told her that it was important for her to experience a past-life regression.

"I have several problems," she said. "Some you can see, and some you can't."

Sutphen could see that Barbara was obviously referring to her excessive weight when she spoke of certain of her problems being easily visible. The attractive twenty-nine-year-old woman carried 225 pounds on a medium-size frame.

Earlier that day, he had observed her during the first two group regressions, trying to be comfortable in two chairs because her weight made lying down on the floor with everyone else too difficult. He could see, though, that she was a deep-level somnambulistic subject, for she had practically fallen off the chairs almost immediately after he had begun the induction process.

During an evening session, Sutphen always tries to do some individual regression work so all the seminar participants may better understand the process. On this particular night, he asked Barbara if she would like to participate in the demonstration. She agreed, and along with eleven others, she joined him on the platform.

Sutphen gave the volunteers the following instructions:

"I want you to think about something in your life that you want to change. It can be any kind of problem, habit, or personal situation.

"In a moment I'm going to hypnotize you; and when I touch each of you on the hand, I'll be talking directly to you and only to you. I will count backward from three to one, and on the count of one, you are going to move back in time to the cause of your present problem—if indeed the cause lies in the past in this life or in any of your previous lives. You will see and relive this situation before your own inner eyes, and thus you will understand the problem and begin to release it."

*   *   *

Once the group hypnosis was completed, Sutphen began to move down the line, touching each subject on the hand, counting backward from three to one, then saying, "Speak up now and tell me what you see and what you are doing!"

In this demonstration, Sutphen always found the individual reactions of the subjects to be filled with surprises, for they are being directed back to the cause of their problems, which, more often than not, is a traumatic situation.

That night a man was crying out in anguish as he relived an ancient battle.

A young woman was reliving the fear of being lost in the woods as a small child.

A middle-aged woman was starving to death in an African village.

When he came to Barbara, she cried out, screamed, and began to shake. Her voice was that of a young girl on the edge of panic: "Oh, no . . . no, no, no! Oh, please, please! Why are you doing this to us?"

Her reaction was too extreme to allow her to continue under the present circumstances of a demonstration.

"Return!" Sutphen commanded, and Barbara's body went limp as she relaxed into a peaceful, hypnotic sleep.

After all of the other subjects had been awakened, Sutphen asked Barbara if she'd like to explore in more detail the prior life on which she had touched so emotionally. But now, he told her, it would be on a one-to-one basis, so he could devote all of his attention to her. Once again, she eagerly agreed.

Sutphen induced the hypnotic trance state again, and Barbara was instructed to the same lifetime that she had visited before. This time, however, it would be a month earlier.

In a few moments, she was speaking in the voice and persona of a twelve-year-old French girl, describing her luxurious home and her perfect life in eighteenth-century France at the time of the Revolution.

When she was moved forward in time, she experienced the arrival of soldiers who had orders to take her family to prison. Numerous humiliations followed, and the young girl was eventually killed by the revolutionaries.

After her death experience in that lifetime, Sutphen directed a question to Barbara's Higher Self: "How have the events in this past life in France related to Barbara's problems today?"

From the depths of her hypnotic sleep and her very soul, Barbara cried out: "Pretty people get hurt! I was so pretty, and they killed me. The only way to be safe is to remain ugly to the world. Then you'll be safe . . . then you'll be safe!"

After she was again awakened from the trance state, Barbara provided additional information about her weight problem. She explained how she had attended the best and most highly recommended weight-loss centers, but she could never shed the pounds. In some cases she had begun to lose a little, then she would go on an eating binge and bring her weight right back to 225.

One well-known specialist had told her that once she found out *why* she psychologically needed to retain weight, then she would be able to keep it off.

"You know you can do that *now*, don't you, Barbara?" Dick Sutphen asked.

"Oh, yes. Now I know I can!" she beamed back.

Lafcadio Hearn observed that for thousands of years the East has been teaching that what we think or do in life really determines the future place and state of our essential substance.

"Acts and thoughts, according to Buddhist doctrines, are creative," Hearn writes in *Kotto*. "What we think or do is never for the moment only, but for measureless time; it signifies some force directed to the shaping of worlds—to the making of future bliss or pain."

Pierre Leroux points out that if we learn to regard the world as a series of successive lives, we may be able to perceive, at least partially, how God, for whom neither time nor space exists, can permit suffering as being a necessary phase that humans must pass in order to reach a true state of happiness that we could not conceive from our mortal viewpoint.

Using Past-Life Regressions to Correct Present-Life Traumas

Benjamin Smith of Port Orchard, Washington, has been involved in past-lives therapy for over twenty years. In addition to conducting workshops in past-lives exploration, he also works individually with clients. In his "other life," he is a real estate appraiser/consultant.

"When I first began to do regressions professionally, I spent a lot of time and energy trying to establish dates, names, and locations of the person being regressed," Ben told me. "Then I discovered that my clients didn't really care if they would be able to trace a particular lifetime. All they were interested in was removing the personal problem that they had come to me for help in solving.

"I then quit worrying whether reincarnation was *real* or not. The important thing to my clients was whether or not they discovered the solutions to their problems. If the solution came from their previous lifetime or from their higher consciousness, it really did not make any difference to them. The important thing was that they found the solution that they had sought."

A Pain in the Back Over a Thousand Years Old

When I asked Ben if he would provide some illustrations of how past-life therapy had produced the answers to some of his clients' present problems, he was quick to oblige me.

"One of the most dramatic has to be Ron's story. He came to me several years ago, complaining of a sharp pain in the lower left side of his back that he claimed to have had since he was about eighteen years old. He had gone to numerous medical doctors, but they had not been able to find any physical reason for the chronic pain."

After getting his client into a relaxed state of mind, Ben asked him to go back in time to the source of the pain in his back.

"He immediately saw himself as a young man of fifteen, working in a field in the time of ancient Rome. He was a farmer's son, and he hated the rural life."

Ben moved the regression along, directing his client to see himself in an important event in that lifetime.

"He went to a time when he had a serious argument with his father. He was rebelling against the life on the farm, and the only out that he could see was to become a Roman soldier."

The past-life regression moved Ron to a scene in that life in which he saw himself as a soldier practicing with a short sword and a spear.

"The next important event in his past life was participating in a battle at about the age of eighteen (Ron's approximate age when the back pain began in his present life). He had just killed an opponent when he felt a pain like fire in his lower left back (the site of the pain in Ron's present life), and he found himself on the ground, looking up at the blue sky and wondering what was happening to him."

Ben suggested that he rise above the scene and see what was going on from that perspective.

"He said that he could see his body lying on the ground with the battle raging on all around him. He felt quite detached from both his body and the battle. He said that all of a sudden nothing seemed very important."

Ben then directed him to go to a place where they could meet with his guides in order to discuss how that past lifetime had impacted his present-life experience.

"His guides told him that in that Roman lifetime he had been impatient to escape the life of a farmer and had wanted to seek adventure. The pain in his back in his present lifetime was to remind him that earthly adventure sometimes had high costs and that everyone must take responsibility for the choices that they make.

"His guides concluded by saying that now that he had made the effort to become more aware in his present lifetime, he no longer needed the painful reminder in his back and he could now release it.

"We then went through a little White Light work, and Ron released the pain—which, as far as I know, has *never* returned."

Releasing the Karma, Rather than the Symptoms

"I believe that once we understand the source of the problem, we can release the symptoms and the Karma that have resulted from a past-life experience," Ben said. "But without knowing the source, we frequently only release the symptoms which can then return in another form until we have effectively dealt with the Karma.

"In the twenty years that I have been involved with past-life regression, I have found—personally and professionally—that by looking at our past lives we are better able to understand why we have some of the relationships and traumas that we have in our present lives, and we can release the Karma that can tie us to relationships and situations that are negative.

"I have found that by going back to previous lifetimes, I, myself, have been better able to understand a variety of lifestyles by *reliving* those lifestyles.

"For example, I had always felt that I had a rather good understanding of homosexuality from my friends and acquaintances in this lifetime who are gay. Then I went back to a lifetime in Victorian England when *I* was gay, and I discovered a whole different perspective on what it is like to be homosexual."

Two Requests from Nadine of El Paso

Ben shared another case of his that dealt with a woman from El Paso named Nadine.

"Nadine and her mother came to me wanting to find out the answers to two questions: 1) Why was Nadine overweight and unable to keep the excess pounds off? and 2) Why was she sexually frigid?

"We were able to answer both questions in one regression. I regressed Nadine to a lifetime in Victorian England when she was a prostitute. But apparently she hadn't been a very good one, and she had starved to death. I thought her mother would fall out of her chair from laughing so hard."

Nursemaid to the Child of an Alien Mother

A third case from Ben Smith's files was quite provocative.

"Darlene, a woman from Albuquerque, had a very special relationship with her daughter. She was convinced that the two of them had shared many life experiences, for when her daughter was eight years old, she had asked, 'Mama, where is the place that was all white?' Darlene had thought about the peculiar question for a while, then replied, 'Do you mean the delivery room when you were born?' To which her daughter quickly answered, 'No, before that. When we were deciding which one of us was going to be Mama this time.'

"Because of her daughter's obvious awarenesses and her own intuitive feelings, Darlene wanted to discover information about the very first lifetime that they had shared.

"The regression took Darlene back to a life in South America—she thought it was in Peru. At that time, the entity that was now Darlene was a servant to an alien female, who she remembered as being very large, but not fat—and about seven feet tall. The alien had had a daughter by a native man, but she was being recalled to her home planet and was unable to take the child back with her. She entrusted the little girl with alien heritage to Darlene—and apparently, she was still caring for her through many lifetimes."

CHAPTER THREE

We Are Souls that Choose Human Bodies

Bettye B. Binder, president of the Association for Past-Life Research and Therapies, has conducted over 3,400 individual past-life regressions and has taught over 15,000 students in workshops and classes since 1980. The author of six books on past-lives, her *Past Life Regression Guidebook* is now in its fifth printing.

Although our personal interaction has regretfully been limited to moments of conversations captured between lectures or workshops on the seminar circuit, both my wife Sherry and I have always felt a warm aura of kindness and goodwill emanating from Bettye.

When I asked her for a recent case from her files that demonstrated the benefits of past-life regression, she quickly supplied me with the following story:

Darrell has told his story to the television programs *Sightings* and *20/20*, and in time I will probably write a more detailed account in a future book.

A native of Toronto, Darrell has lived in southern California for many years. He came to me in 1981 for classes and for private past-life regressions. His presenting problem was terror of drowning in the middle of the ocean. He was not frightened of seashores, swimming pools, or other bodies of water; but he would not venture very far into the ocean because of his fear of drowning there.

In three separate regressions, he discovered that he had drowned in the middle of the ocean in three previous lifetimes. In one, he was a black slave in the South, about 1840, who tried to escape in a small boat that sank due to an explosion on board. In 1940, before the United States entered World War II, he was a young man from Pennsylvania who joined the Canadian Air Force and was shot down over the Pacific Ocean. However, his death on the *Titanic* was the most important experience related to his phobia.

In regression, he experienced being a crew member on the *Titanic*, which sank after striking an iceberg in the middle of the Atlantic Ocean in April 1912.

He was asleep in his bunk when the crisis began. He was awakened and told to go to the boiler room where he worked. It was flooded, so he went to the next available boiler room that was still free of seawater. He and his workmate did their best to get the ship moving, but it soon became evident that the *Titanic* was sinking.

Darrell stayed at his station while the other man went topside to find them space in a rowboat. As is well known, there were not enough boats to save the lives of everyone on board. His friend got on the last one available and left Darrell stranded belowdecks.

When his friend did not return, Darrell went topside. He arrived in time to see his workmate leaving without him on the last boat. He was livid at being deserted. Then the ship began to lurch and dive into the depths. Darrell hung on to the rail, but very soon he became tangled up in the ropes and drowned.

Bettye has had Darrell reenact this regression on several different occasions, both as a demonstration before groups of students and for television. Each time, she said, Darrell has gotten more and more resolution from such explorations of his past life as a victim of the *Titanic* disaster.

"In June 1992, when I regressed him in front of a television crew for *Sightings*, Darrell saw his angels leading him away from his mangled past-life body, and he felt peace and light come over him as he rose toward the heavens," Bettye said. "He also felt deep compassion for the man he had been as he saw the body entangled in heavy ropes on a mast of the sinking ship."

Bettye pointed out that what was most significant about this remarkable case history is how the experience has turned Darrell's life around.

"I remember him as he was fourteen years ago," she said. "He was a timid, withdrawn, fearful young man, whose life and career were going nowhere. He had dreams of becoming an animator for a major movie or television studio, but those dreams were not being realized. His decision to undertake those past-life regressions in the early 1980s began his personal search and strengthened his desire to overcome the fears that had blocked him for so long. He worked hard, and his hard work paid off."

Bettye added that one major indicator of his success was Darrell's desire to confront his terror of drowning.

"One year he gave himself a birthday present of a raft trip down the Colorado River. Yes, the raft capsized. No, he wasn't scared. Darrell said that he knew that he was mastering his fear, and he knew that he would not drown this time."

After she regressed him again in 1992, Darrell's career began to move in an exciting new direction.

"He was hired as an animator on his first major feature movie," Bettye said. "And that's not all. At Christmas 1994, he wrote to me to say that he had been hired to direct an animated feature film. This was a huge career breakthrough and a big step in screen credits."

As a past-life regressionist, Bettye said that the biggest change that she has seen in Darrell has not been his material success, but his emotional and spiritual development.

"He exhibits a sense of peace and happiness that he never knew before he undertook past-life regression. Gone is the fearful, withdrawn young man of the past. Today he is poised and self-assured.

"Darrell has learned lessons that he was unable to learn in the previous past lives in which he drowned, and he is no longer phobic about the ocean. When I look at Darrell today, I see a man who smiles easily and who is doing what he loves most in life. He has gained a spiritual peace for the first time in several lives."

Our Souls Exist in a Multidimensional Universe

In her view of past life exploration, Bettye Binder believes that the key to making reincarnation acceptable in the Western world lies in our culture learning to acknowledge our true identities as souls that exist in a multidimensional universe where time is not limited to a linear construct.

In her article "Thoughts on Time: The Connection Between Multi-Dimensionality and Reincarnation," *The Journal of Regression Therapy*, Volume VII, Number 1, December 1993, Bettye writes that in her more than thirteen years of teaching classes in reincarnation, she has found the concepts of "multidimensionality" and "simultaneous time" to be the most difficult for students born in our culture to comprehend. In her opinion, it is our devotion to the idea of linear thought and our rejection of everything that cannot be perceived with the physical senses that block our understanding of multidimensionality.

When we reconnect with someone we have known in a past life, she suggests the process is very much like continuing an interrupted telephone conversation. "Now, where were we?" we might ask, and then continue talking as if no time has elapsed.

Similarly, to pick up where we left off with memories of past lives, we disconnect from our current routine and remind ourselves where we left off in a past life. In a certain sense, we "hang up the phone" consciously on what interrupted us in order to experience states of awareness that are deeper than our current physical experience. Through the altered state of consciousness that we call "meditation," we can experience what "multidimensionality" and "simultaneous time" *feel* like even if we do not yet understand what the words mean.

Bettye has said that we can best understand how our past lives are currently influencing our present-life experience if we acknowledge that our true identity is that of a soul who has chosen currently to occupy a human body.

A teacher of reincarnation since 1980, she frequently emphasizes in her classes that we don't *have* souls, *we are souls*! "All of us are souls who chose to become human beings, but our human identity is limited to being in this body. The soul is pure energy, and energy cannot be destroyed. The soul's existence is independent of the body it occupies. It is the soul that continues to exist after the human body dies, and it is the soul that reincarnates lifetime after lifetime."

Experiencing an Awareness of the Multidimensional Self

Alicia Caldwell of Georgia lived with her biological mother until the age of three. After that she spent two years in and out of different foster homes until her parents adopted her when she was five years old.

When she was about ten, Alicia began drawing pictures of two houses and a young woman. Although she drew these sketches again and again until they became almost an obsession with her, she had no idea what they meant, at least on a conscious level.

"It was at the age of fifteen that I began to think about death," she said. "I began to question who was God; where did He come from; when did He begin; and when will it all end?

"I found that I really had no fear of dying. The thing that bothered me was the thought of eternity. I could not comprehend it."

Alicia was twenty-four when she had her first out-of-body experience.

"Somewhere in my memory I knew that I had done this before; therefore there was no fear."

She has experienced out-of-body projections many times since, and each time she begins to feel as though she is "fading away."

Everything becomes gray, then turns black. I am no longer aware of my physical being, but I am *very much* aware of *me*. In fact, all of my senses seem to be about 100 times higher.

I find myself in an area that is very dark with what seem to be "stars" all around. I call it my "plateau." It is the most calm, serene place I have ever been. It feels like home to me . . . It feels like the place to which I go to gather emotional and spiritual strength.

When I come back into my body, one thing I remember very clearly is that while having the out-of-body experience, I knew everything there was to know in the whole universe. Even though I don't remember all this wisdom and knowledge, I know that I knew it.

In 1980, when she was thirty-two, Alicia said that her "whole world got turned around"; and when she recounted the story to me in 1987, she still felt as though she was riding "a very fast roller coaster." It was at that time that she began to have memories of things that just didn't fit into her life.

"I remembered such things as riding on a paddleboat, wearing long, old-fashioned dresses, and the names of persons I had never known in my present life," she said.

The name "Marietta" bothered her a great deal. Since she knew that she had been adopted and did not recall very much about her biological mother, Alicia began to assume that Marietta had been her name and that she was experiencing some kind of preadoptive memories.

As time went on, these ostensible memories bothered her to the extent that she conducted a search and met her biological mother, whose name was *not* Marietta. Alicia learned that she had been very ill with pulmonary problems as a child. According to her mother, Alicia had "almost died" on three occasions. But none of these things appeared to have anything to do with the strange memories that haunted her.

Later, with the aid of hypnotic regression, Alicia relived the life of a young girl who was named Sandra Jean Jenkins, who had lived from 1895 to 1914. Marietta was the name of the small town in southeastern Ohio where Sandra Jean had lived.

I have been up there twice in the last year, and I found the family to which Sandra Jean belonged, the home in which she lived, and the cemetery in which she was buried. I have also learned many details about her brief life.

Imagine my surprise when I found that the houses I discovered in Marietta turned out to be the homes that I had started drawing when I was ten years old!

The picture of the girl who I have drawn all these years was Sandra, and I found her standing among her relatives in a "family reunion" picture taken in 1908. She was a suicide.

The reality of Sandra Jean Jenkins was confirmed for Alicia by two geneologists in that area.

"All this is not something that I could have made up," she said. "I was totally shocked. Up until that time in 1980, I had lived in the typical Christian tunnel. I believed deeply what I had been taught: 'You're good; you die; you go to heaven. You're bad; you die; you go to hell.'

"I not only did not believe in reincarnation, I thought it was a word that did not even belong in a proper dictionary!"

It seemed as though when Alicia had found Sandra Jean's grave and discovered that she had been an actual person, not a fantasy, she "just got slapped up alongside the head" with the reality of past lives.

"When I realized what was happening and that what I had been taught was not correct, I had to take everything that I had formerly believed and reassess it. I still have problems at times believing and understanding that [reincarnation] is real."

Then, several months before Alicia sent me her account, she had meditated for the first time.

"I had been taught while growing up that meditation was wrong and evil. However, during this meditation, I met my Guide. His name is Chyamiah (pronounced Hi-a-ma). He is an ancient Israeli."

After her spiritual contact with her guide, Alicia said that she began to write in a language that was totally unfamiliar to her.

"I thought that it might be ancient Hebrew, so on an outside chance, I took it to the Orthodox rabbi here in town. He said that it was not Hebrew, but it appeared to him to be Aramaic. Whenever I pray, I have begun to speak in a language that I don't understand."

Alicia said that the most startling and profound thing had occurred to her only a month before she contacted me:

I had been asleep in my bed, and as I began slowly to wake up, it seemed as though I was streaking forward very fast through a very bright, white light.

Then I saw several planets that were spinning very quickly. They did not look like the photos of the planets that I have seen of our galaxy. One planet in particular came to my attention. It was a very pretty pink and blue.

When I was fully awake, I realized I was very dizzy and nauseated. I raised up on my left elbow and swung my feet out of the bed. As I sat up, I suddenly became aware of the fact that there was definitely someone standing at the foot of my bed. I could see him out of the corner of my eye, but for some reason I could not look directly at him.

Eventually he went away. After he left, the first thought that went through my mind was that he was an "E.T."—an extraterrestrial.

About a week later, while meditating, I saw

a very bright, white light to the right side of my body—even though my eyes were closed.

The light was outside of my body, not within my eyes. At the same time, I felt an overpowering presence from the place from which the light was coming.

Alicia had been writing a letter before she had begun her meditation, so she went to her desk and picked up the pencil to write the message that she felt the Light Being had to transmit to her.

Although she channeled the entity's message with her eyes completely closed, when she opened her eyes to read the communication, she saw that she had dotted all the "I's" and crossed all the "T's" and that not one word ran into another. Among the messages the Light Being transmitted, Alicia shared the following:

Travel the path of the Light. Go toward your destiny of a oneness with the universe.

Tell the children of the Earth plane to look up and to walk wisely, for the growth of their souls is up to them.

Go to the right hand and follow the path of the mission set before you. Teach, teach, teach the growth of the mind so that other souls can grow before the cleansing begins.

While a Priest Gave Him Last Rites, He Was Reliving a Past Life

For nearly thirty years, F. R. "Nick" Nocerino of Pinole, California, has been one of the foremost psychical researchers and teachers in the United States. An internationally recognized authority on the mysterious ancient artifacts known as the "crystal skulls," Nocerino is also an accomplished investigator of haunted houses.

At my request, Nick told of the series of visions that began when he was hospitalized in 1953 with a near-fatal illness. In these vivid past-life recalls, he saw himself as a person intent on punishing all those who committed acts of murder and brutality. Interestingly, the memories continue unabated to this day.

"All of my visions appear to focus on a past life that occurred around A.D. 400 through 445," he said. "I see torture chambers, beheadings, the rack, even dismemberment. I often see myself in hand-to-hand combat with a sword or a knife and sword."

During a severe illness that he suffered in 1953, Nocerino lapsed into a coma shortly after he had been admitted to a hospital.

"My coma proved to be very exciting. While I was removed from the external world, I saw myself as a warrior-priest; and I also appeared to enjoy the role of executioner. It seemed as though I held some sort of very high position that permitted me to enact judgment on violent criminals of all sorts.

"From the time perspective of the coma, it felt as though I had spent weeks—even years—reliving that lifetime. Then a voice out of nowhere told me that I had to leave and go back to the present time to finish my other work.

"I was puzzled. What 'other work'? I kept hearing the words, 'Spread your knowledge . . . spread your knowledge to others.'"

Nocerino opened his eyes and, at the same time, felt agonizing chest pains. He could see his wife Khrys at his bedside, and he told her that he was hungry.

Later, his physician, Dr. Smith, told Nocerino that the medicine that had been previously prescribed for his illness had literally been killing him.

While he was recovering from the illness, Nocerino continued to slip away into his past-life memories—which led to a very bizarre set of circumstances.

"Each time I killed someone in battle or in the torture chamber in my past life, I would open my eyes in the present and see the patient in the bed opposite mine being taken out of the hospital room wrapped in a sheet. Good lord! Was I somehow really killing people in *both* lifetimes?"

Later, when Dr. Smith informed him that he

was getting well enough to be moved to the main ward, Nocerino learned that the room in which he had previously been placed was a kind of "holding" room one step away from the morgue. It was the room where they sent patients they considered "ready to leave this world."

When Nocerino was getting steadily stronger, a priest visited him and admitted that he had been given the last rites on numerous occasions. More than once, the priest said, everyone thought that he had died. The other two beds in that room had a steady turnover of dying patients.

"My name in that past life seemed rarely spoken," Nocerino said, "but I believe that it was Francesco. In one combat by sword, I received a thrust into my chest.

"After I had regained my senses emerging from the coma, I remember screaming that I had a severe pain in my chest. I could see that there was a bandage on my chest, and I became confused, wondering if it was from my wound from the sword thrust in my past life.

"But Dr. Smith told me that he had had to puncture my chest bone to remove some marrow for testing. He told me that I had screamed very loud, and he felt that this was what had broken my coma and began to bring me back to consciousness."

Nocerino concluded his account by stating that to this day he can often become confused with what is or was a scene from his past life. A particular sound or even a change in the weather can bring him visions of himself in that other time period, especially after he has read or heard about a criminal act having been perpetrated.

Reincarnation Gave Her a Deeper Understanding of the Christian Faith

Dr. Gladys McGarey is a medical doctor who employs various concepts from the Edgar Cayce material in her practice at the Association for Research and Enlightenment Clinic in Phoenix, Arizona. On one occasion I asked Dr. McGarey, the daughter of Christian missionaries, how her work with the Cayce readings had changed her basic spiritual beliefs:

My attitude toward life and death, religion and immortality, my basic philosophical platform, probably has not changed in that it is still Christ-centered with a basic Christian foundation. The part that has changed is the addition of reincarnation and the concept that comes from the Cayce material that gives impact and reality to the importance of us as ongoing beings. We are as rays of light and love that are involved in this three-dimensional world.

A lot of the Christian philosophy implies that

when we die, we become immortal. I now believe that . . . we *have been* immortal and when we live we *are* immortal and when we die we *continue* to be immortal. We just happen to be living in a mortal body.

Rather than taking her away from the church, Dr. McGarey told me that the concepts of reincarnation had actually given her a deeper understanding of Christian ritual and the belief structures of the Christian faith. She also said that the concepts of past lives had helped her to be a better physician, because they had enabled her to share responsibility with her patients, "rather than take responsibility from them."

A Case of Karmic Balance

Dick Sutphen told me about a case of his that involved a woman who had received "flashes" and "quick inner visions" while he was conducting a group hypnotic regression. Later, during a private counseling session in his office, the client, Denise Walsh, a formal-appearing, middle-aged woman, said that she had heard herself as a man swearing allegiance to someone or something named "Diocletian," and seeming to curse a certain group of people.

"Could any of this relate somehow to my present problems?" she wanted to know.

Sutphen explained that such a regression session as the one that she had undergone was often a good way for the unconscious to release something that was being repressed or causing hidden anxieties. He asked her if she had ever heard of Diocletian or if the name related to anything in her present life.

After a moment's thought, she shook her head. "No, but I was just fired from my job, and I can't seem mentally to recoup from the shock. I'm going to be in economic trouble very soon if I don't manage to get a hold of myself."

Denise went on to tell Sutphen how she had maintained a position of ever-increasing authority within a large insurance company. She freely admitted that she had enjoyed "using her power," that she was not well liked by other employees. Recently, as the result of an administrative shakeup, she had been assigned to a new supervisor who had taken an immediate disliking to her. A few weeks later, he had fired her.

Sutphen conducted two private sessions with Denise Walsh, and he retrieved the following information from her past-life experience:

In the year A.D. 294, during the decline of the Roman Empire, Denise was a man named Carius. He resided in England as a provincial supervisor under Emperor Diocletian.

Carius's appointment had been made by a special governmental committee, and during a period of revolt by the English people, he found himself in the position of directing large numbers of Roman soldiers. However, Carius did not have a background as a military man, so a conflict soon developed with the officer in charge.

Throughout his administration, Carius had favored excessive cruelty and mass violence as the most effective means of maintaining civil control. The Roman officer, on the other hand, advocated the use of restrictions and the limited use of violent examples to create an environment of hardship and fear, thus achieving the same end result.

Brooking no level of disagreement, Carius negotiated the recall of the officer and his subsequent demotion. The Roman officer who replaced the more moderate military adviser was more than pleased to institute Carius's plans—which resulted in years of bloody rebellion and never-ending turmoil.

While Denise was still in a deep hypnotic state, Sutphen directed her consciousness up into the "Higher-Self" mental realms. This special technique allowed her to tap into the "all-knowing" levels of the superconscious mind. From this perspective, she was able to perceive that she still had not learned to use power correctly. And she saw clearly that until she did, she would continue to be "toppled" by others.

"It is so simple," she said. "I must simply be kind and loving toward all . . . those above me and those below me in authority positions. Then there is no limit to my ability to achieve."

Denise was also able to see that the Roman officer who had opposed her in her life as Carius was the supervisor who had fired her in her present life.

Quite some time after the hypnotic sessions with Denise had been completed, Sutphen happened to meet someone who had worked at the same insurance company during Denise's tenure.

"She was an absolute tyrant," the man said. "Denise expected everyone in that office to do her bidding, including those above her. When she started her usual routine on her new boss, he just eliminated the problem by getting rid of her."

Sutphen saw Denise's case as an excellent example of karmic balance, cause and effect. "She told me that she was going to find another position, and she felt certain that she would never again misuse authority. I didn't hear from her after our two sessions together, so I hope that her past-life regression proved to be a positive tool for greater understanding, thus helping her to create a new and positive personal reality in her present life.

"By the way," he added, "the historical facts of Denise's regression were all valid. Consciously,

Denise had never heard of Emperor Diocletian; and she had never studied the Roman Empire in any depth during her school years."

"A lifetime may be needed merely to gain the virtues that annul the errors of man's preceding life," said the novelist Honoré de Balzac. "The virtues we acquire, which develop slowly within us, are the invisible links which bind each one of our existences to the others—existences which the spirit alone remembers. . . ."

CHAPTER FOUR

Meeting Judas and Other Soul Archetypes

In the thirty years that I have worked with the challenge of exploring past-life soul memories, it has often seemed as though the great majority of the men and women who came to seek counsel from me had literally created their own demons in the forms of phobias and fears that they had permitted to consume their energies and their spirits. Far too often, these individuals appeared to have made a conscious choice to be a part of the "scandal" rather than the "glory" of the universe. So many of them had developed attitudes of despair and desperation, and they seemed all too willing to fall into hells that they had fashioned out of their individual realities.

As my research has progressed, I have come

more and more to see that the great value of exploring one's soul memories is to provide the troubled individual with an opportunity to acquire practical tools by which he or she might begin to solve current-life problems and begin to build a more positive future. In order to implement such a process, I created a number of techniques that were designed to enable my consultees to examine those alleged past-life experiences that they needed to know about for their good, their gaining, and their spiritual evolution. In each exercise—most of which involve the visualization of an angelic guardian or spirit teacher—I seek always to promote self-esteem, rather than ego, and a true knowledge of the soul's mission on Earth, rather than self-indulgent expression. I will share many of these successful techniques in appropriate places throughout this book.

On occasion, I have had a consultee come to me with preconceived notions of having lived an illustrious life as an Egyptian High Priestess, an Indian Chief, or the ruler of another planet; but by placing the person in an altered state of consciousness and gaining access to the angelic guide or the Higher Self, the individual has been able to see what he or she really needed to learn for true soul evolution, rather than transient ego gratification.

And then there have been those occasions when I found myself dealing with men and women who had fallen into the snares of self-deception that abound in the world of metaphysical metaphors and spiritual similes.

The Great Soul Archetype Phenomenon

In the summer of 1982 when I was lecturing at a metaphysical conference near Los Angeles, a very earnest young woman I'll call Tammy asked me if I might provide her with some guidance. When I indicated that I had a few minutes before my next lecture, she lowered her eyes in shame and confided to me that she had just learned through a past-life reader that she had been Judas in a prior existence.

"You mean *the* Judas?" I questioned, wanting to get this straight. "Kissing Jesus on the cheek, betraying him in the Garden of Gethsemane, receiving the pieces of silver. *That* Judas? Judas Iscariot?"

She nodded her head sadly. She was, indeed, *that* Judas.

I knew that it would avail me nothing to inform her how many alleged incarnations of Judas, Peter, Mary, Joseph—and, yes, even Jesus of Nazareth—that I had met during my research into past lives. I could see that the young woman was truly upset. And from her perspective, understandably **so**, since she apparently believed the pronouncement of the past-life reader.

How, she asked me, could she possibly be able to work off so much Karma this time around?

Then, answering her own question that she could not possibly shake off the stigma of the deceitful disciple in her present incarnation, how *many* lifetimes, she wondered, might it take to wash off the stain on the soul of the entity who had betrayed the Master?

After I had asked her a few gently probing questions, I learned that Tammy had been feeling very guilty lately for having betrayed a boyfriend with a new lover. In fact, she admitted after a few more questions, she had throughout her young life established something of a pattern of feeling guilty for what she assessed as her weaknesses of the flesh.

I assured her that odds were truly against her being the actual present incarnation of *that* Judas, but I acknowledged that she might be acting in the vibratory pattern of the Judas Archetype. In point of fact, she had been a "Judas" in the eyes of her former lover, and she had felt the pain of his accusations of betrayal. In her own words, she had "sold him out," and she confessed that she had been "bought" by another's seductive promises of a better life.

I discussed archetypes and metaphysical metaphors with Tammy for as much time as I could spare before my next lecture, and I think I may have convinced her that she was not the present incarnation of the "damned for all time" betrayer of Jesus. There is, however, a rather bizarre sort of perverse romanticism associated with the character of Judas that may have countered any of my arguments of spiritual common sense.

During an earlier conference in Arizona, I had occasion to observe the Great Soul Archetype Phenomenon at work in full force.

A number of men and women attending a week-long seminar on reincarnation and past-life recall had felt a pleasant rapport immediately upon their first meeting of one another. This sensation of companionable warmth soon led to small, informal gatherings at their hotel rooms where group meditations produced some very startling channelings. Higher guidance indicated certain other men and women who were also attending the conference should be invited to participate in these private meetings.

By the third evening of the seminar, there were fourteen select members in attendance at the special group meditations being held separately and apart from the other participants in the organized lectures and workshops.

By the fourth evening, it was revealed that the fourteen select members in attendance were the present physical incarnations of the twelve disciples, Mother Mary, and in the small, pert frame of a young woman, Jesus—all reborn, all reunited wondrously at a past-lives conference in Arizona.

During the course of earlier research, I had previously witnessed such holy reunions. While investigating UFO contactee groups throughout the United States and Canada, I frequently discovered that extraterrestrial entities had revealed to the inner circle that they had lived together before as Jesus and the twelve disciples. On more than one occasion, they had found themselves just one member short, and they welcomed me with great warmth, as they recognized me to be Philip or James or whomever had been missing.

Far from assessing such past-lives revelations as blasphemous expressions of ego, I have come to regard such prior-life discoveries as little more than impromptu pageant plays. In my follow-up investigations, I have found that most of the men and women who had enacted the archetype of a disciple or of Jesus for a few days or a few weeks generally feel rather embarrassed by their prior-life presumption when the effects of group enthusiasm begin to wear off. Later, really none the worse for the experience—and sometimes pleasantly more aware—they resume their present lives in the real world with more conviction to fulfill their Earth missions properly than they might have had before the role of holy figure was offered to them.

And before you become too judgmental of these folks, consider the fact that each year at Christmas we have little boys and girls at Sunday schools throughout the Christian world dressing up in bathrobes and tinfoil halos to carry makeshift shepherds' crooks and wisemen's gifts to two of their classmates who are temporarily personifying Mary and Joseph to the hushed delight of the audience of beaming parents. The baby Jesus is very often a dime-store doll—or in some instances a lightbulb—which, depending upon one's point of view, may be no less a sacrilege than having a sincere past-life meditator assume the role for a few days.

On the other hand, it would truly be cause for some concern if the little impersonator of Mary should come to believe that she would one day bear the Son of God, just as it would create ripples of potential tragedy if our adult pageant players should assume their auspicious roles of divinely appointed disciples on a more permanent basis. When one refuses to relinquish the archetype several days after the houselights have dimmed, so to speak, then professional assistance may be required to deflate the pumped-up psyche.

The Ancient Doctrine of Reincarnation

Reincarnation is an ancient doctrine, ancient even at the time of the Greek and Roman empires. Plotinus, in the *Second Ennead,* writes that reincarnation is ". . . a dogma recognized throughout antiquity . . . the soul expiates its sins in the darkness of the infernal regions, and . . . afterwards. . . . passes into new bodies, there to undergo new trials."

Pythagoras is reported to have been the first of the Greeks to teach the doctrine that the soul, passing through the "circle of necessity," was born at various times to various living bodies.

Plato alludes to reincarnation in many of his essays, and he seems to be speaking of the ethics of Karma in Book X of *Laws* when he says: "Know that if you become worse, you will go to the worse souls, or if better, to the better; and in every succession of life and death you will do and suffer what life may fitly suffer at the hands of life."

Cicero's *Treatise on Glory* concedes that ". . . the counsels of the Divine Mind had some glimpses of truth when they said that men are born in order to suffer the penalty for some sins committed in a former life."

The chief theological work of the Hindus, the

Upanishads, expresses the doctrine of rebirth in the poetic imagery of a goldsmith who takes a raw piece of gold and shapes it into another, more beautiful form. "So, verily, the Self, having cast off this body and having put away ignorance, makes another new and more beautiful form."

The *Koran,* holy book of the Muslim faith, states that ". . . God generates beings and sends them back over and over again, 'til they return to Him."

St. Augustine asks the eternal question in his *Confessions*: "Say, Lord, to me . . . say, did my infancy succeed another age of mine that died before it? Was it that which I spent within my mother's womb? . . . and what before that life again, O God, my joy, was I anywhere or in any body?"

In his *Exhortations to the Pagans,* St. Clement of Alexandria does more than echo St. Augustine's plaintive query of whether or not we had an existence prior to the one before we entered our mother's womb.

"We were in being long before the foundation of the world," St. Clement declares. "We existed in the eye of God, for it is our destiny to live in Him. We are the reasonable creatures of the Divine Word; therefore we have existed from the beginning, for in the beginning was the Word . . . Not for the first time does He show pity on us in our wanderings; He pitied us from the very beginning."

The original pragmatic Yankee, Benjamin Franklin, saw the whole matter of past lives and rebirth as a matter of very practical cosmic recycling: "When I see nothing annihilated [in the works of God] and not a drop of water wasted, I cannot suspect the annihilation of souls, or believe that He will suffer the daily waste of millions of minds ready-made that now exist, and put Himself to the continual trouble of making new ones.

"Thus, finding myself to exist in the world, I believe I shall . . . always exist; and, with all the inconveniences human life is liable to, I shall not object to a new edition of mine, hoping, however, that the *errata* of the last may be corrected."

The quick wit of Voltaire expressed the mystery of reincarnation succinctly when he said, "It is no more surprising to be born twice than once; everything in Nature is resurrection."

In *Religion and Immortality*, Professor G. Lowes Dickinson presented his view that reincarnation offered ". . . a really consoling idea that our present capacities are determined by our previous actions and that our present actions again will determine our future character."

Such a philosophy, Professor Dickinson observes, liberates people from the bonds of an external fate and places them in charge of their destiny. "If we have formed here a beautiful relation, it will not perish at death, but be perpetuated, albeit unconsciously, in some future life. If we have developed a faculty here, it will not be destroyed, but will be the starting points of later developments. Again, if we suffer . . . from imperfections and misfortunes, it would be consoling to believe that these were punishments of our own acts in the past, not mere effects of the acts of other people, or of an indifferent nature over which we have no control."

CHAPTER FIVE

Will the Real Mark Twain Please Stand Up?

In the early 1980s, I engaged in an interesting correspondence with Faye Frost, a freelance writer and novelist, who had devoted more than twenty-five years to her part-time avocations of hypnotherapy and psychical research. Then, in one of her letters, she shared her personal belief that she had been Samuel L. Clemens, Mark Twain, in her prior-life experience:

I recently returned from a trip to Hartford, Connecticut, where I went through the Twain home for the first time in this life. . . .

The look on the tour guide's face (and on the face of the ticket seller) was worth a thousand words. They looked as though they had seen a ghost. . . .

The ticket seller said that for just an instant, she had seen the face of Mark Twain as if superimposed on mine.

I knew every nook and cranny of that house. . . . It was like coming home. Even now, when I look at the color brochure with the photos of each room, I feel the tears starting to flow. I really loved that house . . . I had never been to Hartford . . . but I drove directly to the house without the aid of a map and without asking questions. . . .

I have also visited [Twain's] childhood home in Hannibal, Missouri, and it is exactly according to the recurrent dreams that I had as a young child in this life in Shreveport, Louisiana.

I answered Faye's most interesting account by telling her that she could not have been Mark Twain, because I had been Clemens/Twain in one of my past lives.

Seriously, I told her, as a boy who seemed "born" to become an author, I, too, for a time, had become so obsessed with Twain that I had nearly convinced myself that I was his present incarnation.

I had to admit, though, that as a child of ten, I had seen Frederic March's interpretation of the writer in *The Adventures of Mark Twain* (1944); and Twain's white mane of hair and mustache also reminded me of my dear paternal grandfather.

On the other hand, on numerous occasions, members of my lecture audiences had approached me and, claiming to be "authorities" on Mark Twain, asserted how much I reminded them of the late author-lecturer. They cited my manner of speaking, my habit of pacing while I spoke, my penchant for blending humor with the serious points of my presentation. Since Twain died in 1910, I never really understood exactly how these people had acquired such intimate knowledge of the man's personal idiosyncrasies unless they were basing their assumptions on Hal Holbrook's marvelous impersonation in his famous one-man stage presentation of an evening with Mark Twain.

At the same time, I informed Faye, I had met at least three other sincere individuals, one of whom was a respected college professor, who were quite certain that they had been Mark Twain in prior lifetimes.

Perhaps, I suggested, there were a number of us who had somehow been born in the *frequency* of Mark Twain and were therefore destined to become writers. In like manner, potential physicists might now be born in the Einstein vibration; dancers, in the Isadora Duncan or Fred Astaire vibration; a mystic in the Joan of Arc frequency, and so on.

To put it another way, many individuals may somehow be very close to being the same kind of receptive channel for higher energies who are using certain archetypes as models by which to inspire us. And when that Divine transmission is beaming forth its message of guidance, men and women of similar sensitivity may pick up its broadcast—and at the same time, may also receive impressions of one another.

I think something of this nature occurs when strangers approach one another and remark: "You seem so familiar to me. I believe that we must have shared a past-life experience."

The reason that we occasionally seem so familiar to one another need not necessarily be because we have shared a past-life experience. The actual reason may be that we are simply very close to being the same kind of receptive channel.

To fashion an illustration, I might be Soul Vibration MTESEO20001 and you might be MTE-SEO20002 or MTESEO20003; but we may be very close to being the same spiritual frequency. Quite naturally, therefore, we might know a great deal about the inner workings of one another, although we have never met on the physical plane. And we might certainly know very much on one level of consciousness about the archetype that has been utilized by higher energies to provoke and inspire us.

* * *

I was very pleased when I received Faye's response to my metaphysical musings:

It is interesting that you [Brad] yourself have wondered if you were Mark Twain in another life. My question is: Why not?

Perhaps all of our concepts regarding reincarnation have been too constricted. Why not five Mark Twains—or a hundred thousand?

Using your archetype idea, that would not necessarily make any of them false. (My husband suggested 100,000 Attila the Huns causing havoc today.)

In other words, we would have a *generic* Mark Twain packaged under many different labels, and with many combinations of ingredients. But the generic base would still be Mark Twain.

People I have encountered who, under very deep hypnosis, recall and relive lives as "great personages out of history," all have that sense of *mission*. It would be interesting to find out if all the Mark Twains and Catherine the Greats have pretty much the *same* mission. In other words, a great spirit divides itself into many segments.

Of course, there is always the idea of spirit possession . . . and of the atmosphere as a psychic storage battery, so that "tuned-in" people are picking up energy patterns still active. . . .

*   *   *

Faye went on to explore the concept of a "great spirit dividing itself into many segments" by stating that she had also identified with the possibility of having been Joan of Arc in a prior-life experience. Once Faye met another woman who had insisted that she had been the Maid of Orleans, and the similarity of their present lives had been "beyond belief."

We were both born in Texas and raised as only children by our grandmothers in Shreveport.

Both born in the same year, but different birth signs. She was Cancer; I'm an Aquarian.

Both our grandmothers were called "Big Mama."

Both our mothers worked in the retail clothing business.

Both our fathers were interior decorators.

Our maiden names were similar—Wood and Ward.

Both of us had married first at the age of nineteen to men of Italian descent.

Both of us had two boys and one girl.

Both of us had lived in Buffalo, New York, and in Florida.

Both of us had remarried in the same year to men of similar disposition.

Both of us were freelance writers.

If there's no coincidence, to what extent did a generic Joan of Arc affect us both?

The Psychiatrist and the Reincarnationist

British psychiatrist Dr. Denys Kelsey quite openly stated his belief that reincarnation is a fact. Because of his acceptance of the cycle of rebirth, Dr. Kelsey endeavored to show his patients how they might begin anew at any given moment.

"The work that I have done has convinced me that it is occasionally possible for a subject to recall experiences that were felt centuries before their present incarnation," Dr. Kelsey once told reporter Douglas Neale of United Press International.

Belief in the doctrine of rebirth may have come somewhat easier to Dr. Kelsey than it does to the average psychiatrist, for he was married to the remarkable Joan Grant, an author who claimed to be "25,000 years old" and to have soul memories of thirty prior-life experiences. Ms. Grant wrote seven popular historical novels without doing a bit of research, yet none of the material in her books has ever been successfully challenged by skeptical scholars. To the contrary, a good deal of the material in her books that was considered controversial at the time of publication has since been validated by archaeologists and historians. Always, when queried how she could have acquired such knowledge, she attributed her accuracy to memories of her past lives.

Winged Pharoah, the novel that Joan Grant wrote in 1937, described her life as a woman pharoah in the first dynasty of Egypt, 4,000 years ago. Once when she was asked to comment on the books's almost biblical style, she replied that the words had just come out that way: "I believe that technically the style is called five-foot iambic. I never did any research at all. I knew nothing of Egypt; yet Egyptologists have been unable to fault the book. [Critics have said] I couldn't possibly have made it all up, that I must have experienced it all to write it in such detail."

In his *The Destiny of Man*, J.G. Fichte argued that since humans are not a product of the world of sense, their existence can never be attained in that world. Humankind's ultimate destination, it would seem, lies beyond time and space and all things connected with the world of sense.

Creativity and Past Lives

Creative people often seem to be given glimpses of their past lives. The old records, journals, and biographies of artists, poets, and writers are filled with such allusions.

Among notable contemporary artists who admit to having been inspired by "memories" of unknown origin, I noted with great interest that Broadway lyricist Alan Jay Lerner said that the first-act ending of his musical *Brigadoon*, which features an outdoor wedding ceremony in the Scotland of the seventeenth century, seemed at first to have sprung spontaneously from his mind. Several years later, when Lerner was in London, he came into possession of a book entitled *Everyday Life in Old Scotland* and found "his" marriage ceremony word for word.

Lerner's later musical success, *On a Clear Day You Can See Forever*, openly declared the lyricist's fascination with the subject of reincarnation. The storyline tells of a Brooklyn model who is regressed to an earlier life in eighteenth-century England.

In explaining his motivation for writing a musical play about such a controversial subject as rebirth, Lerner said [*Atlantic Monthly*, November 1965]: ". . . I had become increasingly outraged at all the pat explanations psychoanalysis was throwing up to explain human behavior. I was becoming more and more disgusted by the morality of psychoanalysis—that we are living in a world where there is no more character and where everything is behavior; that there is no more good, it is all adjustment; that there is no evil; it is all maladjustment.

"Psychoanalysis has turned into a totally unsatisfactory religion which gives no life hereafter, and no divine morality to live by.

"And so I began to think . . . I would find a way of saying I don't think that we are all that explainable; that much of us is still unknown; that there are vast worlds within us. . . ."

Bettye B. Binder, president of the Association for Past-Life Research and Therapies, believes that awareness of our past lives can either facilitate or block the way we live our present-life experience, because in her view time is "multidimensional."

The past influences the present whether or not we are aware of its influence upon us. . . . What we usually think of as "here and now" is simply what we consciously experience at the moment. So when we recall a past life, it becomes "here and now" to our conscious mind at the time of our past-life exploration.

A Simple Exercise in Spontaneous Past-Life Recall

As a simple experiment in spontaneous past-life recall, lie or sit in a comfortable position and permit yourself to relax as completely as possible. Have some paper and a pen ready to take notes. Take a comfortably deep breath, hold it for the count of three, then slowly exhale. Repeat this breathing process two more times.

Consider the following questions and give your answers as quickly and spontaneously as you can:

In moments of reverie ever since I was a child, I have often thought of living in another time, another place.

When was that time?

Where was that place?

What sex was I?

What was my physical appearance?

What was my skin color and/or ethnic group?

What work did I do?

How many brothers and/or sisters did I have?

Did I marry?

Did I have any children?

What was my religious preference?

Were my life situations generally happy or unhappy?

What were my greatest conflicts?

What were my greatest triumphs?

How did I die?

What was the most important lesson that I gained from that lifetime?

Did anyone from that lifetime come with me
to my present-life experience?

What life mission am I to attempt to complete in my present-life experience?

CHAPTER SIX

Researching Impossible Memories

My initial correspondence with Loring G. Williams, which began in the spring of 1967, developed into a friendship and a research relationship that lasted until his death in 1975. Together we investigated dozens of cases suggestive of reincarnation, and we taped hundreds of hours of men and women dramatically providing details of what seemed to be their past-life experiences.

My contact with Williams began just as I was leaving my teaching career and embarking on a full-time exploration of the strange and the unknown. He sent me a package of past-life regressions that he had taped in his hometown in New Hampshire; and as I listened to the tapes, if I was not immediately convinced of their validity, I was enormously impressed with the dramatic intensity of the phenomenon.

Although I was quite certain that he had not established a New England repertory company of superb amateur actors, I found it difficult to accept the hypnotist's assessment that all of these subjects were indeed reliving prior lifetimes. At that time, even though I had always been fascinated by accounts of past lives, my position toward the question of rebirth was rather cautious. While I believed firmly that we humans and our psyches were something other than physical things, I was at that time still reluctant to set aside completely my religious bias against reincarnation. At the same time, I felt compelled to continue to research the subject because of certain "impossible" memories of my own, an irritating number of cases that held up under the most exacting analyses, and because of the great thinkers, who, through the ages had professed their belief in the ethics of Karma and the reality of reincarnation.

"Once You Hear the Genuine Emotion, You'll Be Convinced!"

"You must hear for yourself these people reliving their past lives," Loring "Bill" Williams told me. "You must hear them suffering through the death experience, being reinstated on Earth through the birth experience. Once you hear the genuine emotion in those voices, you'll be convinced that these subjects are truly reliving former lives—and not simply acting out fantasies."

As I learned—first, from Williams's correspondence; later, from firsthand observation—the subjects who are regressed to ostensible former life experiences actually relive those times in a manner that surpasses simple remembering. They feel the same pain; they see familiar objects; they use colloquial expressions, although not always with an expected accent. They either do not see or do not recognize anything modern. Instead, they see only the period of time to which they have been regressed. If the regressionist calls their attention to anything contemporary, they may seemed dismayed, for they are actually living temporarily in another era.

At first I supposed that such an emotionally draining process would cause the subjects distress after they had been brought out of the trance state. But I saw that there was no such effect, because the subjects were left with no memory of what had taken place. If the subjects should request a tape recording of their session, they might later find it interesting or entertaining, but they will not feel that it is really them on that tape.

As with any potent instrument, one must exercise caution and common sense when working with hypnosis. There is always the possibility that the subject may relive a very traumatic experience. If this should occur, the regressionist must know his or her technique well enough to recognize—by facial expressions and other signs—such psychically supercharged areas and to carry the subject quickly through or around such experiences.

Loring G. Williams considered hypnosis—altered states of consciousness—to be the "key that unlocks the door" to great progress in the field of psychical research. "Contrary to widespread belief, hypnosis is not a sleep," Williams explained. "It is a trance state in which the words of the hypnotist reach beyond the subject's conscious to his unconscious. The hypnotist then communicates directly with the unconscious mind."

Survival after death and the nature of death itself are questions that have been pondered by humankind's greatest minds. In the midst of his terrible sufferings, Job wanted to know the answer to the age-old query: "If a man dies, shall he live again?"

The search for the Great Answer continues in many ways and is conducted by many sincere seekers. I found among these spiritual pilgrims, soft-spoken, Yankee-practical Bill Williams, whose method of exploration was to ask his subjects, at the count of three, to journey back through time and space.

George Field Volunteers to Explore the Unknown

In 1965, George Field, a fifteen-year-old neighbor of Loring G. Williams, decided one evening to sit in on the weekly sessions that the high school teacher–hypnotist had been holding in his home. During these meetings, Williams would regress volunteers to past-life experiences in the hopes that he might find a subject whose story could be checked out and verified.

Williams had soon found out that such a search is not an easy one. Many subjects when regressed are hazy about such details as their full names, their parents' names, the year in which they were born or died. Others, though they may go into vivid detail, describe an existence so long ago—or in so remote a place—that verification is out of the question.

Young George proved to be an ideal subject for hypnosis. He went easily into a trance and was amenable to hypnotic suggestion. Within a short time, he was describing a prior-life experience that had taken place in North Carolina at a time in history that would be near enough to check out.

While in a deep trance state, the New Hampshire teenager "remembered" a life as "Jonathan Powell," who had lived from 1840 to 1863. He recalled that his father's name was Willard and that his paternal grandmother was named Mary. He could not remember the name of his mother.

According to Jonathan, his father worked a small farm and labored in the nearby tin mine. The Powell family were Quakers, ministered to by a traveling parson named Brown.

In a series of hypnotic sessions, Williams continued to move George/Jonathan back and forth in the time sequence of his lifetime. As the teenager spoke, a tape recorder caught every word; so, if possible, Williams could later substantiate the actual physical existence of Jonathan Powell.

When Williams took Jonathan up to his last day in that incarnation, the North Carolina farmer was in the nearby village of Jefferson in Ashe County, busy loading potatoes for the "damn Yankee soldiers." According to the disgruntled Jonathan, the soldiers were willing to pay only a few cents a bushel for the crop that he had worked so hard to harvest from the soil. He cursed the men strutting around in their gray uniforms.

Williams queried the entity on this point. If the soldiers were wearing gray, then they must be Southerners, not Yankees.

"Naw, they ain't Southerners," Jonathan said firmly. "They're Yankees!"

But the farmer was becoming more concerned with the soldiers' motives than their identities. They were surrounding him. They wanted five sacks of potatoes, but they said they would pay only ten cents a bushel. The stubborn Jonathan told them to keep their money.

Then, suddenly, George/Jonathan began to cough and to make terrible sounds of pain.

Williams spoke softly to him, reassuring him that all was well, that he would be able to speak without pain.

After the hypnotist had removed the awful hurt, Jonathan told him that he had been shot in the stomach by the plundering soldiers because he would not take their "damn money." The entity complained that the wound still "hurt a little."

Williams progressed the mortally wounded farmer ahead five minutes in time. When he asked Jonathan what he felt at that point, the entity answered that he could feel nothing.

"Nothing," Jonathan repeated in a puzzled tone of voice. "I can't feel anything. I can't see darn thing."

The hypnotist spoke again, soothingly, to calm the panic that showed in Jonathan's speech. "There's nothing to fear. On the count of three, you will come back to the present time. . . ."

Returning to Jefferson with Jonathan Powell

Loring Williams was now most eager to travel to Jefferson, North Carolina, to substantiate Jonathan's story and to attempt to confirm the physical existence of the personality from whom he had learned the details of an apparent previous Earth life. Williams, his son, Jack, and George Field decided to make a camping trip to Jefferson just as soon as school was out for the summer.

Williams was fortunate in that an old army buddy had become a minister and was serving a congregation in Watuga, Tennessee, while living in Johnson City, just a short distance from Jefferson. The clergyman's backyard would provide the expedition members from New Hampshire with a base of operations from which to conduct their field research in Jefferson.

Williams had enthusiasm and high hopes. He had visions of Jonathan/George running about the village, recognizing familiar landmarks, leading them to his mother's grave, falling weeping upon his own burial place. Then it would be a simple matter to proceed to the courthouse and find all the records that would substantiate the previous existence of George Field in the actual person of Jonathan Powell.

Things did not quite work out that way.

As the trio approached Jefferson, George claimed to have strong feelings that he had been there before.

Williams placed the teenager in a deep-trance state and regressed him to 1860. As George became Jonathan once again, Williams cautioned him to pay no attention to automobiles or other modern contrivances. The hypnotist did not wish to take any chances of frightening Jonathan or in distracting him with any puzzling artifacts of the twentieth century.

When Jonathan opened his eyes to Jefferson village for the first time in over a hundred years, he was completely dismayed.

"Picture yourself, if you can," Williams said, "going back to your old neighborhood after an absence of a hundred years. There are all new houses and streets, and you're trying to locate your own backyard."

The Discovery of Mary Powell's Deed

When the investigators visited the Ashe County courthouse in Jefferson, they were disappointed to learn that the county had not recorded births and deaths before 1921!

However, there had been a registry of deeds.

On page 430, Volume A, Williams and the two boys found the copy of a deed in which a Stephen Reed had conveyed to a Mary Powell a parcel of land in 1803.

This discovery excited the three investigators very much. Jonathan had named a Mary Powell as his paternal grandmother. In 1803, Mary Powell would have been about the right age to be buying farmland.

The trio became even more sure of their research when they were told that Powell was a very uncommon name in that area.

The register of deeds referred Williams to a local historian who might be able to tell them the geneology of the old families of Ashe County. Williams called the historian and made an appointment with her for that afternoon.

Jonathan's Remarkable Interview with a Reluctant Historian

When she learned the purpose of their expedition into North Carolina, the historian went on record as saying that she did not believe in that sort of thing. In spite of her strong objections to the idea of reincarnation, she did agree to offer what help she could; and after she had listened to a tape recording of one of George's regression sessions in New Hampshire, she had to confess that she was most impressed with "Jonathan's" knowledge of Ashe County.

Williams regressed George to Jonathan as the personality would have known Ashe County in 1860.

"Remember to keep your questions in the present tense," he cautioned the historian. "To Jonathan, it is still 1860."

The historian questioned Jonathan about a total

of twenty-five personalities and events who figured in the history of Jefferson village from that period of time. The regressed personality claimed to know fifteen of them, many in detail.

For example, when the historian asked if Jonathan could remember Joshua Baker, the high sheriff of Ashe County, he gently corrected her and said that Baker had been high sheriff ten years before, in 1850. Later, after referring to the old county records, the historian learned that this was true.

When the historian asked about the drowning of Colonel George Bower, she expressed some surprise that Jonathan seemed astonished to learn of the prominent gentleman's death. Once again, though, after she checked her records, she found that Colonel Bower had drowned in *1864*, four years later than the time sequence in which the regressed entity was transiently dwelling.

The guileless historian often phrased her questions in a manner that could easily have encouraged either conscious or unconscious lying or guessing on the part of the interviewee, but Jonathan answered all queries in a straightforward manner, regardless of the historian's innocent prompting. For example, when she insisted that he must have known the "rich old merchant Wall," Jonathan said that he did not, but that he knew Samuel Wall—and he proceeded to give the correct location of his home.

Although she was at first reluctant to participate in such an experiment, the historian eventually entered wholeheartedly into the spirit of things; and she chuckled and nodded enthusiastically throughout Jonathan's vivid characterization of one of the wealthiest members of Jefferson society *circa* 1860.

Later, when Jonathan indicated extensive familiarity with the historian's *own* ancestors, she seemed truly satisfied that she had not embarked on a foolish chore.

In addition to the astonished historian's confirming Jonathan's basic knowledge of the people and events of Jefferson *circa* 1860, she substantiated his memory that there had been a circuit-riding Quaker preacher named Mr. Brown. Although she could find no records of an established Quaker meeting place, she readily conceded that a group might have met in private homes.

Evaluation of Jonathan's Hits and Misses

In going over transcripts of the sessions with the historian, Williams and I asked ourselves why it was that Jonathan seemed to know more of the obscure members of the village than he did the prominent, the wealthy, and the clergy.

Part of the problem may have lain in semantics.

When the historian asked Jonathan if he *knew* such and such a prominent person, the poor dirt farmer may have taken the question literally. A hand-to-mouth farmer does not really *know* his banker, his preacher, his magistrates, or other wealthy or influential citizens—even in a village as small as antebellum Jefferson, North Carolina. In a number of instances, Jonathan did, in fact, state that he *knew of* a certain individual. Perhaps this manner of speaking should have been picked up on and clarified during the actual interrogation, and Jonathan should have been told that *identification,* rather than a claim of intimate knowledge, was all that was being asked of him.

Since the historian's interview of Jonathan Powell was much more than a yes-or-no quiz, it is impossible to provide the percentages on the entity's hits or misses. The regressed personality was asked about a total of twenty-five persons or events in Jefferson *circa* 1860. Jonathan readily admitted having no knowledge of some of them, but he did know something about fifteen of the individuals and items on which he was queried. Over 50 percent of his "hits" mentioned such correct details as financial status, physical descriptions, children's names, location of residences, and the construction of homes.

On the one hand, it would be correct to say that George/Jonathan should not have known any details about Jefferson "villie" in the North Carolina of 1860. At the same time, he could have answered yes to every question. The fact that he offered correct details in his answers would seem to rule out the possibility of guessing. His misses only prove that he, a reclusive young farmer, did not know everyone in Jefferson. In our opinion, he gave enough detailed and correct responses to make the possibility of chance very remote.

Here are some selected excerpts from the historian's interrogation of George/Jonathan:

Historian: Were you acquainted with the rich merchant Wall?

Jonathan: No. I knew Samuel Wall.

Historian: All right, Samuel Wall lived in Jefferson at that time; but you didn't know the rich old merchant?

Jonathan: I didn't know him. [We feel this response is rather significant. Jonathan could easily have agreed that he knew the "rich old merchant Wall." Instead, he correctly identified Samuel Wall, who also lived in Jefferson at that time.]

Historian: Were you acquainted with David Worth?

Jonathan: Let's see. David Worth. He lives down in the center of the villie. Yeah, I know he lives there, but I've never met him. [The historian conceded that Jonathan had accurately placed the location of Worth's residence in the village.]

Historian: Did you know Jonathan Baker?

Jonathan: Yeah, he lives down in the center of the villie, too. I've met him quite a few times. He's got a lot of money. And he always talks about it, too! I think he's got quite a few slaves. [The historian chuckled and nodded throughout Jonathan's enthusiastic recounting of the wealth of Jonathan Baker.]

Historian: Do you recall meeting any members of the Ray family?

Jonathan: They have a girl about my age. I think her name is Mary.

Historian: And she never married?

Jonathan: No, I don't think so.

Historian: (Chuckling) Aunt Polly.

Jonathan: Who's Aunt Polly?

Historian: Aunt Polly was Mary Ray. Her nickname was Aunt Polly. [Jonathan seemed to know the Ray family quite well, for he became excited at the mention of their name. In 1860, Mary Ray would have been just his age. The fact that he was unfamiliar with the "Aunt Polly" nickname is hardly surprising. At the time of his death, Mary would not really have been old enough to have given up hope of marriage and to have earned the "Aunt" title awarded to spinsters in those days. Mary Ray or Aunt Polly was a well-known member of the historian's own family.]

Historian: Do you remember Gideon or Isaac Lewis?

Jonathan: (Becoming excited) Isaac! Yeah, yeah, he lives down the road from me about a mile or so. I don't know his wife, but I do know Isaac. He's come up to see me before. [Jonathan apparently knew Isaac Lewis, where he lived, his profession, and his marital status.]

Historian: No doubt you are acquainted with James Eller.

Jonathan: Not personally acquainted, but I've seen him.

Historian: What does he look like?

Jonathan: Well, he's fairly tall, and he has black hair. I never looked closely at his eyes, but I think they're brown. I've heard a lot talked about him, but I've just seen him. Never met him.

Historian: You probably remember when Colonel Bower built his brick home.

Jonathan: Yeah, it was about ten or twelve years ago. It was in the forties. [This was a good hit. The Bower home was built in 1848. Since Jonathan was speaking from the year 1860, his "ten or twelve years" hits the date right on the nose.]

Jonathan Expertly "Takes Some Snuff"

Williams recalled a humorous incident that occurred while he was driving around Jefferson with George and Jack. The boys asked him about the "snuff" that they had seen for sale in numerous places in the village. In New Hampshire and throughout the United States in general, the "taking of snuff" is practically a lost "art." When Williams explained to the boys what little he knew of this particular use of tobacco, he learned later that he had confused snuff with chewing tobacco.

That afternoon, while shopping at a supermarket, Williams bought a tin of snuff as a souvenir for each of the boys. A bit later, as the three of them were riding around the countryside, Williams regressed George to Jonathan in the hope that he might recognize some landmarks and locate the site of his farm. But then another idea occurred to the hypnotist.

"Do you like snuff, Jonathan?" he asked.

"I sure do!"

Jonathan had a little trouble getting the snuff out of "that kind of a box," but once he had the tobacco tin open, he set about "blowing" it in a skilled and expert manner.

Williams was startled. He had never seen anyone sniff tobacco up the nose before. It took him a few puzzled moments before he remembered an article that he had read long ago that described this manner of "taking snuff" to have been a popular use of tobacco in generations past. But it was still amazing to him to watch someone actually "sniffing" tobacco. It was an accomplishment that obviously took considerable practice and experience—not to mention a strong, well-conditioned nose. He knew that the New Hampshire teenager had never before seen someone "take snuff," and he was certain that George Field had never tried it.

A Letter from Jonathan's Great-Niece

The difficulty in substantiating such an obscure and nondescript life as that of Jonathan Powell in a manner that will offer satisfactory proof of reincarnation to everyone is probably an impossible task.

Williams always felt that one of the most significant aspects of the case was Jonathan's description of his death. He claimed that he was shot to death by Yankee soldiers in gray uniforms because he refused to accept their low pay for his potatoes. Even the most casual student of Civil War history knows that the northern soldiers wore blue uniforms. Furthermore, Williams's research established the fact that there were no Yankee troops in that part of North Carolina in 1863.

"Once again, though," Williams said, "Jonathan was right. The local historian said that at that time there were bands of renegades who came down from the North, using the war as an excuse to raid and plunder. They could very well have been dressed in gray, because they would have stolen their uniforms."

As more attention was directed to the case, Williams received a letter from a woman who claimed to be the great-niece of Jonathan Powell and who cleared up a number of items that were unclearly stated by the personality of Jonathan:

He [Jonathan Powell] was killed by the Yankees, so my father said; but he didn't know any details at all about how he was killed.

Willard Powell was Jonathan's brother. Jim Powell was his father [Jonathan stated that his father's name was Willard and that he could not remember having a brother]—and he was redheaded or sandy-haired. All the family had blue eyes. We never knew what became of Willard or his family.

. . . My mother often talked about the Quakers and they would spend the night with her family. . . . There was no Quaker church.

I haven't done any research . . . but a lot of those eastern Tennessee men fought for the South. That could have been some of them in the gray uniforms who killed Jonathan, or it could have been the renegades.

As for what the case of Jonathan Powell proves, Bill Williams rightly stated that each person who studies the records of the investigation will have to decide for himself or herself. The skeptic will proclaim that nothing has been proven. The believer will proclaim that we have a clear case of reincarnation.

Williams always tried to remain objective about the case, but he could not resist drawing his own conclusions that there was much more at work than coincidence could account for. He believed that after the passing of over 100 years, they had found as much evidence for the reality of Jonathan Powell as anyone could hope to find for someone who lived a short and unremarkable existence. He was convinced that Jonathan Powell had truly lived in Jefferson, North Carolina, from 1834 to 1863. After knowing Jonathan and visiting Jefferson with him, Loring G. Williams could believe nothing else.

Portrait Projection Exercise

As a simple experiment, try this elementary exercise in spontaneous past-life recall.

Select a time when you know that you will not be disturbed for at least twenty minutes to half an hour. Take two or three comfortably deep breaths and either sit back or lie down. Relax as completely as possible. You might play some soft, tranquil, "floating and drifting" type of music. Just be certain that your musical selection does not contain any lyrics that may distract you.

Imagine yourself standing before a large door of softly glowing white light. See the door opening. You know that this white light is holy and sacred and that it will surround and protect you from all negative energies. Picture yourself walking through the doorway and into what appears to be some kind of magnificent museum that is filled with articles and objects from earlier periods of history.

As you walk farther into the museum, you understand that it is dedicated to artistic representations of the soul and its various expressions throughout all of time.

As you turn a corner, you suddenly confront a full-length portrait that you *know* within your soul essence is a portrait of you in a prior-life experience. You *know* in every fiber of your being that this is a portrait of you as you appeared in an important past-life experience.

Visualize the portrait before you. Even though the figure may not greatly resemble you in your present-life experience, you are certain beyond all doubt that it is the expression of your soul in a past life.

Is the figure male or female?

How is the figure dressed?

What historic period of time suggests itself to you as you see the clothing the figure wears?

How is the figure posed? What is the figure doing?

From what you can see, is there any clue that tells you in which field of thought, endeavor, or accomplishment the figure excelled?

Study the portrait carefully. Feel yourself becoming one with the portrait. Feel yourself breathing life and warmth into the portrait.

See yourself beginning to relive an important event from that lifetime.

In what country or place did you live?

In what era of historical time did you live?

What was your greatest ambition in that lifetime?

What did you most want to accomplish?

Now visualize a scene of conflict, stress, or strife from that lifetime.

See if you sense or perceive anyone from your present-life experience who may have fought or struggled against you in that prior lifetime.

Now see if you sense or perceive anyone from your present-life experience who championed you or supported you in those past scenes of conflict and chaos.

If you recognize anyone who opposed you or who worked with you from that past-life experience, take a few moments to contemplate why you have come together again in your present lifetime.

Scan that lifetime and see clearly the faces of those who were your parents in that life experience.

If it is for your present good and gaining, see clearly if you had brothers and sisters . . . a spouse . . . children.

Did you achieve your goal or mission in that lifetime?

How did you die?

What was the most important lesson that you learned from that lifetime?

What situation would you most like to redo from that lifetime?

What pattern of behavior would you least like to repeat?

What talent or ability would you most like to regain?

Now visualize yourself once again outside of the portrait. See yourself once again in the museum that is dedicated to artistic representations of the soul throughout history.

Visualize yourself walking back to the glowing door of white light. See yourself stepping through the light, returning to the present.

Take a few moments to reflect on any information that you have received that may seem especially relevant to any present-life situation. Take any notes that you feel may contribute to your good and your gaining as an evolving soul.

The Lessons of Schoolhouse Earth

Author Berry Benson once phrased the dogma of reincarnation in the analogy of a small boy who enters school and is placed by his teacher in the lowest class and is charged with learning these lessons: Thou shalt not kill. Thou shalt do no harm to any living thing. Thou shalt not steal.

So the little boy grew into a man. He did not kill, but he became cruel and he stole.

And the end of the day "when his beard was gray; when the night had come," the teacher noted that although the student had not killed, he had failed to learn his other lessons. "Come back again tomorrow," the teacher said.

When the new day dawned, the pupil returned to school and was placed in a higher class because he had accomplished one lesson.

Then the teacher gave him these lessons to learn: Thou shalt not cheat. Thou shalt not steal. Thou shalt not do harm to any living thing.

Again the boy grew to a man. He was careful to do no harm to any living thing, and he tried his best not to be cruel; but he stole from his neighbors and he cheated to accomplish his own ends.

At the end of the day, "when his beard was gray; when the night had come," the teacher recognized that the student had learned to be merciful, but he had failed to accomplish the other lessons. Once again, the student was told to return on the morrow.

So it may be with us. We may all be learning some lessons and getting failing marks on others in Schoolhouse Earth.

Jesus admonished all those who heard his words to be perfect even as God is perfect. Is it possible to achieve such perfection in a single lifetime?

It would seem more than just to allow souls to return again and again, until all the "lessons" have been learned, before they are made to stand to judgment and are examined as to whether or not they are worthy of attaining eternal life in God Consciousness—or be shut away from God's grace.

CHAPTER SEVEN

Exploring Layers of Consciousness

Throughout the years of his research, Loring G. Williams determined what he believed to be an average of approximately eighty years between lifetimes.

On one occasion, I asked "Bill" what he felt happened to the soul after the physical death of the body.

"I think that there are several layers of consciousness," he replied. "What we call physical life is only one layer—not necessarily the bottom one—and when the body dies, I think the soul first rises to a level of consciousness that is very closely related to our physical world. When the soul is there, it can still see what's going on in the physical world; and in some cases it may be able to make contact with people who are on the physical plane of existence. Such instances may explain some 'ghost' phenomena and some spirit communication.

"I had one subject tell me that he could recall a period after the death experience in which he 'floated' above the graveyard and occasionally went into town to visit his brother, but the man was never receptive. Once the subject said that he mustered enough psychic energy to knock over a lamp in an attempt to attract attention, but he gave up when the cat got the blame!"

In Williams's opinion, a soul remains on this lower level for varying lengths of time, depending on the manner in which the physical body died. In his own research, he found that those entities who died an early or a violent death tended to stay on the lower level longer than those who died of natural causes.

"The next step in soul progression would seem to be what the entities described merely as 'floating,' being unable to see what's going on in the lower levels," Williams said. "Subjects always seem very calm at this level.

"A higher step, I would assume, is when the soul describes itself as doing nothing. This may be the final stage before rebirth. All this is theory, of course."

The Divine Law of Compensation

I wanted Williams's opinion about Karma, the Divine Law of Compensation.

"Karma is difficult to pin down when you are doing regressions unless you know a lot about your subject's background and you are able to explore a number of regressions with the same subject.

"In those cases where I have known something of my subject's history or have been able to learn something of his or her background and have been able to get good detail on several of his or her past lives, I have been able to see a definite pattern of Karma being played out."

Did he agree that the law of compensation, "what ye sow, so shall ye reap," seemed to be in effect?

"I believe so. Maybe Jesus wasn't trying to be as mystical as some interpreters of the Bible say he was. Maybe when he said that man must be born again, that's exactly what he meant. Just plain, 'you must be born again,' *period*.

"Likewise, his admonition to lay up treasures in heaven rather than on Earth certainly becomes extremely meaningful in the dogma of Karma. The life you live on Earth becomes your treasure; and the way you live your life is what counts, not how many worldly possessions you can accumulate."

Divine Mind Knows No Evil

I had more questions for my colleague in past-lives research.

"Do you feel that when Jesus told us to 'be perfect even as our Father in heaven is perfect,' that he was referring to a spiritual progression in which one's spiritual lessons continue until the soul reaches the point where it can be absorbed into the Divine Mind? And what about Divine Mind? Do you believe in God?"

Williams answered that if anything, his research into past lives had strengthened his belief in God. "I believe that God is a force that is *in* everything and a *part* of everything."

Did he perceive this force as benevolent or impersonal?

"Both. It's an impersonal force because it isn't out to do any particular favors for any particular person, but it's a benevolent force because it knows no evil."

Didn't he also recognize an evil force?

"Not in my opinion. Evil is a relative thing. There is no cold, only an absence of heat. There is no evil, only a lack of good. The reason that bad things happen to people is because people don't allow the full expression of the God force in their lives. When we shut out this force, we are left with what we call evil."

Eliminating Fears of Death and Dying

Without appearing negative or nonsupportive, I wanted to ask Bill if he hoped that all his years of regressions and follow-up substantiation of various cases would eventually *prove* the reality of reincarnation to the skeptical.

"Probably not," he answered frankly. "I doubt if reincarnation can ever be proved to the satisfaction of everyone. My work has provided me with personal satisfaction. And it seems to have helped some people eliminate their fear of death and dying."

Do Humans Ever Return as Animals?

I asked Bill if he had ever found any evidence of transmigration in his research.

"No, in my experience, humans always seem to return as humans."

But did he think that animals might have souls?

"Possibly. But they have their own levels. If they did not have *something* immortal within them, then why have so many people seen that ghost cat in our home?"

The Law of Karma and Personal Responsibility

I told my friend that one of the criticisms of the doctrine of reincarnation that I heard most often had to do with the concern that its concept of rebirth would offer people a spiritual crutch.

"If reincarnation became a more acceptable philosophy in the Western world, do you think that the great masses of people will begin to feel that they no longer have to worry about what they are doing in their present lives because they will have another chance to make things right in a future existence? Will the 'weaker brethren' say, 'Well, I'll be reborn a hundred times, so I can raise some hell in this life and make it up in the next one'? Or, perhaps even worse, might the despondent commit suicide to escape the problems in their present life so that they can hurry on to the next one?"

Williams chuckled at my presentation of objections to the doctrine of reincarnation. "Well, you know, Brad, a lot of folks feel that way right now. A lot of people feel that they can go out and raise hell as long as they become contrite in their old age and make some kind of expiation before they die. If reincarnation should ever become well accepted in the West, I believe a true understanding of Karma would prevent folks from 'sowing' a lot of things that they might not care to 'reap.'

"My personal belief is that nobody ever gains anything by suicide. The chief reason someone commits suicide is because he has a problem he feels he cannot face. In accepting the dogma of reincarnation, people would come to realize that if they did not face their problems in this life, they would still have to face it in some other life. If anything, such a philosophy would probably decrease suicide.

"Once people have been made responsible for their actions and have been made to learn that they are going to have to come back to set their own road straight, they are going to want to face up to their problems and get them over with."

If Reincarnation Is True, Why Do We Not More Easily Remember Our Previous Lifetimes?

Dr. Gladys McGarey told me that her friend, Rabbi Herbert Weiner, is fond of telling the following Hassidic tale:

A soul, waiting to be born, sees a preview of his new life flash before him. Then he is told that he must choose whether or not he wishes to be born, for choice is a man's sacred gift from God.

If the soul decides to be born, the Angel of Forgetfulness touches him in the center of the upper lip to seal in the memories—and he comes into the world. This is why we have an indentation in the center of our lip.

Forgotten Memories Still Influence Us

When an English clergyman spoke against reincarnation and concluded by stating that such alleged preexistences could have no moral meaning simply because men and women were unable to remember anything about them, Dr. Leslie Weatherhead, minister of London's City Temple, answered:

"So if some drug were given to [the clergyman] blotting out the memory of his youth, any indiscretions of that youth could have 'no present moral meaning'! He forgets that they would just as effectively have made him and molded him to be what he is, as if he remembered them. A judge is not often ready to excuse a prisoner of all moral responsibility if he asserts that he can't remember anything about it now!"

Dr. Weatherhead reminded the cleric that no one can consciously remember his very earliest years, yet any psychologist will stress the importance of such a period in our development and will convince us of the effect that this period had on us.

"The childhood incidents happened," Dr. Weatherhead commented, "not to another, but to us, and though now forgotten, determined many of our present reactions to life. The very pattern of adult life is a form of stored memory. We do not need to remember mental impressions to be influenced by them."

A Whole Rosary of Lives Threaded on One Personality

Sir Arthur Conan Doyle carefully considered the question of why more people did not remember more of their past lives and expressed his opinion that such remembrance would ". . . enormously complicate our present life and that such existences may well form a cycle which is all clear to us when we come to the end of it, when perhaps we may see a whole rosary of lives threaded upon one personality."

Forgetfulness Can Be a Blessing

Gustave Geley, a tireless explorer of the vast inner worlds of the psyche, saw the fact that the vast majority of men and women have no memory of their past lives as ". . . a great a blessing as ignorance of the future . . . If the commonplace man had but a flash of this knowledge, he would be dumbfounded by it. His present errors and anxieties are as much as he can bear . . . Remembrance of the past could but impede present effort."

An Inner Awareness that We Are Eternal

In Book V of his *Ethics*, Benedict de Spinoza reflected that even though it may not always be possible for all people to remember their previous lives, all humans have within them an inner awareness that they are eternal. We are able to perceive that our mind is eternal ". . . insofar as it involves the body's essence under the category of eternity; and that this, its existence, cannot be defined by time or interpreted by duration."

Casual Gleams of Memory and a Revelation of the Past

Professor William Knight once remarked that forgetfulness of past lives may be one of the conditions of an entrance into a new stage of existence.

"The body, which is the organ of self-perception, may be quite as much a hindrance as a help of remembrance," he stated. "In that case, casual gleams of memory, giving us sudden abrupt and momentary revelations of the past, are precisely the phenomena we would expect to meet. If the soul has preexisted, what we would *a priori* anticipate are only some faint traces of recollection surviving in the crypts of memory."

Past-Life Companion Exercise

Lie or sit in a comfortable position and allow yourself to relax as completely as possible. As background music for your scenario, you might want to play the soundtrack of a romantic motion picture. The only caution is to avoid music containing lyrics that are likely to distract you from the goal of exercise.

Take a comfortably deep breath, hold it for the count of three, then slowly exhale. Repeat this procedure three times.

See before you a lovely circle of glowing white light. You know that this is a holy and sacred light that will protect you from all negative energies. You know that you can step into the circle of light and life and receive knowledge of a past-life companion that will be for your good and your gaining.

Visualize yourself stepping through the circle of light. See now that you have emerged in a favorite place of yours. Perhaps it is on a blanket on the beach. Perhaps it is on a flat rock beside a lovely mountain trail. Or on a park bench feeding the pigeons. You are wherever you choose to imagine yourself, and you have a companion with you.

Focus on this companion. Is the companion male or female?

Study the color of hair, eyes, and complexion of your companion.

Watch your companion's facial expressions, posture, body movements.

Are you relaxed with your companion?

Is your companion relaxed with you?

If there is an instant rapport between you, take a few moments to learn why you feel so much at ease with each other.

If there is veiled hostility or distrust between you, take a few moments to contemplate the origin of such feelings.

Really focus now on your companion's face. Have you known this companion before in your present-life experience, or is the companion only a vaguely familiar stranger?

If you have visualized a person whom you know from your present-life experience, take a few moments to go with your feelings. Who might this person represent to you?

If you have visualized your companion in contemporary clothing, begin now to move deeper into your soul energy, deeper into the light. See your companion in clothing that you think more perfectly suits him or her. Permit this clothing to come from any period in history. Do not place any restraints on the flow from the light that may now be coming to you.

Now visualize yourself with your companion in another time, another place.

If your prior selection of beach, mountain trail, park bench or wherever feels significant, however, stay with that environment.

Imagine yourself taking your companion by the hand as you face a circle of friends. Now make an introduction along the following lines:

*   *   *

"Dear Friends, I would like you to meet my companion, [give the first name that comes to you]. We were together in [name a country] in [the year]. Our relationship was [say the first thing that comes to you—lovers, marriage partners, business partners, siblings, comrades-in-arms, whatever].

"Together we faced [name a situation of stress or conflict]. We shared some bad times [reflect on some] and good times [enjoy positive memories].

"Our life together as companions ended when [remember the circumstances—death, separation, a move, whatever].

"The most important lesson we learned together was [recall why you lived that past life together]."

Now see yourself once again stepping into the circle of light and life and returning to your present life. Take a few moments to reflect on your past-life companion and to take whatever notes you may feel are relevant to your greater understanding and awareness of a larger reality.

In Volume 9 of the *Collected Works,* Carl G. Jung comments that rebirth of the psyche is not a process that we can in any way observe.

We can neither measure nor weigh nor photograph it. It is entirely beyond sense perception. We have to do here with a purely *psychic* reality, which is transmitted to us only indirectly through personal statements. One speaks of rebirth; one professes rebirth. . . .

. . . I am of the opinion that the psyche is the most tremendous fact of human life. . . . The mere fact that people talk about rebirth, and that there is such a concept at all, means that a store of psychic experiences designated by that term must actually exist.

Rebirth is an affirmation that must be counted among the primordial affirmations of mankind. These primordial affirmations are based on what I call archetypes. . . . There must be psychic events underlying these affirmations which it is the business of psychology to discuss. . . .

CHAPTER EIGHT

The Higher Self-Healing of Helen

Dr. Russell C. Davis, editor of *The Journal of Regression Therapy,* has been practicing past-lives therapy for nearly forty years. Although he at first was quite skeptical toward the reality of former lifetimes, his encountering of cases that produced facts and evidence that could be validated eventually made a believer out of him.

In answer to my request for a case of past-life therapy that accomplished the solution of a present-life problem, Dr. Davis generously provided me with the following account:

"The Healing of Helen: A Case of Higher Self Healing of Present-Life Problems Through Past-Life Exploration."

Introduction

Before presenting the case of Helen, it might be useful to the reader to address a couple of important underlying assumptions upon which my approach to past-life regression work is based. First, a determination needs to be made whether the purpose of the session(s) is to conduct research or to be primarily therapeutic in nature. A research approach attempts to arrive at a body of factual data—names, dates, places, events—which could then be validated through historical records and other external methods. When therapy is the primary motivation, verifiable factual information plays a secondary role. The focus is upon whether or not the past-life experience helps the client to affect a desired change, *not* to determine the historical accuracy of the experience itself. (Though I would hasten to point out that sometimes it is possible to achieve both.)

A second important useful assumption is that the client may not *consciously* know what s/he really needs, *i.e.*, the stated purpose of wanting to undergo the experience may not be what the client actually requires at that time. Underlying this second assumption is an understanding that there is a part of the client that does know precisely what is actually needed, regardless of what rationale has been developed by the conscious mind.

In a Christian sense, one refers to an eternal part of a person's existence, calling it one's "soul." Freud, in attempting to define the complexities of the human mind, came to the conceptualization of that portion which functioned as a repository of understandings which lay beyond the realm of conscious awareness. He called it the "subconscious." Many "new age" thinkers refer to one's "Higher Self."

Call it what you will, the concept of an *eternal* part of oneself that moves from lifetime to lifetime is fundamental to conducting past-life regressions. This is the very core of the person that is accessed during the experience and in which is stored that collective awareness of what is and what was. Over the years, I have come to call this "the part of us that knows and understands," and it is this element of the person that I address during the regression experience. In essence, in conducting a past-life regression, this "part of one which knows and understands," the "Higher Self," is asked to reveal to the client's conscious awareness information and understanding about a past life (or lives) and what its meaning is to the present.

Typically, when a client seeks a regressive experience, s/he comes with a specific question or goal in mind. Time and time again, it has been my observation that if the client's Higher Self is asked to provide what s/he *really* needs at that point in time, the client is then given answers and insights far more relevant and meaningful to the individual than those questions or goals which precipitated the initial consultation. Thus, over the many years that I have conducted regressions, I have come to rely completely upon the wisdom of the client's Higher Self.

To illustrate this point, let us consider Helen (not her real name), a pleasant and friendly middle-aged woman with a history of unsatisfactory relationships with men, who called to request an appointment to "explore any past-life connections" between herself and her current present-life boyfriend. That relationship, like all of her previous present-life relationships with men, was stormy and unfulfilling.

Helen arrived promptly at the agreed-to time and, during the intake session, it became quickly apparent that although she had not undergone a past-life regression, she had a general understanding of how it worked and was eagerly looking forward to the experience. As was my custom, I did a normal intake procedure, doing a case history of the client followed by information and discussion about the process itself.

As a therapist who has used PLT as a modality for a good number of years (actually starting back in the late 1950s), I have found it very helpful during the initial intake to collect a case history, and also to discuss candidly and thoroughly the topics of hypnosis *per se*, and past-life regression therapy specifically, establish the client's goals, and discuss the process—how we would proceed, etc. This approach seems to be extremely beneficial in setting the tone and in preparing the client.

Session One

Helen easily entered a hypnotic state. She was then guided through the process of cloaking herself with a protective aura. At this stage, it is my normal custom to establish ideomotor responses (a "yes" finger, a "no" finger and a "I don't know" or "I don't want to answer" finger, all of which would allow for nonverbal communication with the client's Higher Self). Once this was accomplished, I asked her Higher Self for permission to ask questions. Once this permission had been granted (by the movement of the "yes" finger), I said that Helen wished to explore her past-life connection(s), if indeed there were any, with her current boy friend. Again, as is my practice, I added a simple statement, asking Helen's Higher Self to reveal whatever was important for Helen to know at this time. [Note: In conducting a past-life session, I do not suggest or lead. I only question or ask].

Helen lapsed immediately into a past life which,

judging from her description of the countryside and her own clothing, was clearly set in one of the low countries, probably Holland, and, from a historical perspective, probably sometime between the seventeenth and nineteenth centuries. She described herself as a teenage girl who was being pursued by an ugly old man across an open field surrounded by canals. Well into the emotional aspect of the experience, she described her pursuer's facial features, grimacing and distorting her own face in a mock semblance of his.

He quickly caught up with her, tied a rope around her legs, and attempted to rape her. She tried to scream, and he placed his hands over her mouth to stifle her calls for help. She felt her neck pressed against a rock in the field and, as she struggled to free herself, her attacker pushed his hands against her mouth with such vigor that her neck, pressed against the rock, was broken by the pressure and she died. I gently assisted her spirit to move into the Light and there, with her "guides," she reviewed her life.

When questioned whether or not the attacker was her present-life boyfriend, she responded that she thought he was not. At this point, we were approximately forty-five minutes into the regression and, although we had not yet established any apparent answers to the initial question concerning a possible past-life connection between Helen and her present life boyfriend, I asked her Higher Self if there was anything else important for

Helen to know this session. The ideomotor response was "no." Then asked if it were time to bring Helen back to present time and place, the ideomotor response was clearly, "yes."

Once back to a full state of consciousness, Helen was asked what she remembered and how she felt. She was very moved by the strong emotions of the experience, had excellent recall of the events, and was able to provide a significant amount of additional data about both the events and her attacker. Her descriptions were very vivid.

She then made an interesting observation: although she had *not* mentioned it prior to the session, she now revealed that she had two long-term problems that had vexed her since childhood and which now, viewed in the light of her regression, seemed to be explained. First, as long as she could remember, she had been unable to tolerate anything around her legs and was, indeed, even unable to sleep with her legs under the covers. Second, for virtually as many years, she had suffered from an undiagnosed "painful neck." According to Helen, she had sought help from many physicians, chiropractors, massage therapists, and others, all to no avail. There appeared to be no physical reason for the continuous pain in the neck and no relief from its discomfort.

Session Two

Helen called about a month later, requesting a follow-up regression, the purpose of which was, once more, to explore any past-life connections with her current boyfriend, with whom the relationship was still stormy and unsatisfying. Upon her arrival, Helen explained in excited terms that she was now able to sleep with her feet under the covers and that her neck pain had abated to a significant degree.

The induction was conducted in a manner very similar to the first session, and once more, her Higher Self guided her to an experience, this time in the American West during the "cowboy era" of the late 1800s. Once again, Helen found herself the victim of an intended rape by a group of young toughs, this time in the town livery stable. The blacksmith, her friend, attempted to stop the rape and was killed for his efforts. Helen was choked and hanged by the rapists. As in the first regression, she was a victim of a rape attempt and was killed by having her neck broken.

Again, her descriptions of the event were vivid and detailed, despite the emotional impact of the abreaction. After guiding her through the post-death experience into the Light, her Higher Self indicated there was nothing else to be learned that day.

Helen and I discussed in some detail the experience and the similarities between it and the first regression. Further, we noted that her present-day boyfriend did not seem to figure into the experience.

As she left, Helen laughed and said, "Well, I seem to come here with questions and I leave with answers to questions I didn't even ask. . . . But they seem more important to me now!" She resolved to leave it to her Higher Self to reveal to her what she needed to know, rather than to insist on answers to preconceived questions.

The Follow-Up

About one month later, she returned for a third session, this time bringing her boyfriend with her. Before undergoing what turned out to be the first of several fascinating joint regression sessions with her boyfriend, she was delighted to report that *she now had absolutely no symptoms of neck pain and continued to be able to sleep with her feet under the covers.* She was even able to tolerate a blanket wrapped around them as she sat in her favorite chair.

One must remember that the primary purpose of her sessions was therapeutic in nature, rather than for research, *per se*. The emphasis was on seeking answers and affecting positive change, *not* in establishing verifiable empirical data concerning specific names, dates, and places. To that end, the sessions with Helen, and later those with her and her boyfriend, were extremely successful in that she was able to extinguish a phobic reaction to having anything around or over her legs and achieved a complete alleviation of a long-term unexplainable (at least from a medical perspective) painful neck condition. Follow-up contacts with Helen over the ensuing months indicated that these changes remained stable and that she continued to be free of both the old phobic symptoms and the neck pains.

Those joint sessions with her boyfriend, occurring as they did at irregular intervals over the ensuing months, did, indeed, reveal several past-life connections between them and established several reasons for their present-life strife.

Referring to the case in personal correspondence, Dr. Davis commented that in many ways, the story of Helen's present-life boyfriend was an even more interesting story:

"He is, in this lifetime, a simple farmer totally devoid of any sophistication or conscious understanding of anything beyond his own cornfields. Yet, under regressive hypnosis, he was able to provide a substantial body of highly detailed information about a life as an animal tender in the Roman coliseum and another as a simple field worker called to labor in 'the great crystal-domed city.' He described that city—a product of a technologically very advanced civilization—in detail from his perspective as a 'simple worker.' While he, as an unsophisticated worker, was unable to provide a name for the city/civilization, one could easily speculate that it might have been Atlantis!"

CHAPTER NINE

The United States of Atlantis

A young woman from Springfield, Massachusetts, recalled a prior-life experience as "Dionne, an Atlantean priestess":

I lived in the women's temple and was the high priestess at the time of the destruction of the temple. I sent out envoys to what is now Ireland, Spain, and South America to search for a place in which to escape the coming holocaust and to establish a women's temple. These missions were too late and did not succeed. The temple in Atlantis was destroyed by irresponsible use of the great crystal [a legendary energy source of the lost continent].

James, an administrative systems analyst, said that in spite of an orthodox religious training from earliest childhood, he seemed to know that he had lived before in ancient Atlantis:

As a child, I resented anyone telling me that Atlantis was a myth. One of my lifetimes there was spent as a high priest in a temple, assisting people to find themselves and to use their lives to good advantage. My interest in the use of color, both industrially and in the domestic environment, may be a carryover from that life experience.

Leonard, a high school teacher from Detroit, has always believed that he was a scientist in Atlantis:

Before I started kindergarten I was repairing old radio and television sets. I got good grades in math and physics without ever really cracking a book. I just seemed to know about scientific things. In Atlantis, I know that I worked with unusual forms of energy. I believe strongly that I will one day remember more clearly some of the super technology of the lost land and share it with the people of today.

If you make a serious study of past-life research, it will not be long before you begin to make the acquaintance of sincere men and women who firmly believe that they have experienced prior-life times in Atlantis. Whether that fabled land of might and mystery really lies slumbering beneath the oceans or whether it has never risen above the aqueous depths of our dreams, it has stamped an indelible impression upon the collective unconscious of humankind.

While my extensive research into the puzzle of our prehistory has led me to conclude that civilization on Earth has been cyclical and that there have been highly evolved human or extraterrestrial cultures before our present epoch, the Atlantis that rises most often in past-life regressions seems more closely aligned to the mythos of the lost continent envisioned by Edgar Cayce, the famous "sleeping prophet" of Virginia Beach. Cayce, thought by many to be the greatest clairvoyant and prophet since the days of apostolic revelation, depicted the panorama of Atlantis in over 650 life readings given over a period of twenty-one years. During that span of time, the information he channeled was amazingly consistent. Never once did he confuse a date or jumble events he had previously ascribed to a particular era in Atlantean history in readings given years before.

Cayce's history of Atlantis is divided into three broad eras: the First Destruction, the Second Destruction, and the Third, or Final, Destruction.

Students of Cayce's Atlantis readings have

placed the time of the First Destruction at approximately 50,000 B.C. At this time, according to his channeling, Atlantis was a continent; and the seismographic disturbances were minor compared to what was eventually to come.

The Second Destruction, thought to take place about 28,000 B.C., was much more violent, succeeding in breaking up the land mass into five major islands.

The Final Destruction of Atlantis, which plunged the mighty civilization beneath the waves, is said to have occurred around 10,000 B.C.

The Advent of Souls on Earth

Consistent with the first chapter in the biblical book of Genesis, Cayce declared that physical life was already pursuing its evolutionary path on Earth before the arrival of human beings. Furthermore, when those entities that would express humanhood first appeared on the planet, they were in soul form, rather than sheathed in physical bodies. Unhindered by the limitations of a material form, these souls were capable of projecting themselves into other expressions of life. They could inhabit the stalk of a plant or the body of an animal.

The purpose of the soul in entering these material forms was to experience creation, which, as a purely spiritual entity, it could not accomplish without the medium of physical senses. Cayce stated that the five principal racial types of humans occurred simultaneously on Earth because that number represents the five senses, or the five attributes, through which physical and spiritual consciousness may be bridged.

In appearance, Cayce described the souls as being rather in the nature of thought forms, able to push themselves into various shapes. However, by endlessly and carelessly projecting themselves into different forms of matter, they eventually discovered that their ability to project *out* of matter was becoming weaker and less effective. Gradually, materiality hardened around these souls, and they found themselves caught fast in a physical form.

Occurring at the same time was the division of the sexes. According to Cayce's entranced teachings, the soul is androgynous—that is, it incorporates both the male and the female principles. It was in the continent of Atlantis, Cayce channeled, that sex came into being, due to the separation of these two principles.

The physical human forms on Atlantis embodied the red race. According to the Cayce readings, these people developed at a much more rapid rate than the other four races. The souls that projected into the Atlantean land were quicker at learning how to manipulate the forces manifest in their environment.

The combination of projection into animal forms and the arrival of sex produced some very strange bedfellows, and the offspring of these unions were frequently grotesque mixtures of human and animal traits. There were great differences of opinion concerning the nature of these "things," and the fate of the bizarre entities remained a central issue throughout the history of Atlantis, dividing the two rival groups that soon developed.

The Conflict Between the Children of the Law of One and the Sons of Belial

The struggle between the Children of the Law of One and the Sons of Belial continued throughout the successive destructions of Atlantis. According to the Cayce readings, the final destruction was the result of actions taken by the Sons of Belial, who destroyed themselves as well as their opponents with their insatiable desire for knowledge and power.

The beginning of this classic conflict between good and evil dates back to that primeval time when the souls split into two separate sexes and took on physical embodiments. The readings indicate that the material encasement of souls was the result of their own self-indulgence and self-aggrandizement. Through misuse of their creative powers and by their interrupting the evolutionary pattern of Earth, they were now made subject to its laws. They were now forced to live in a physical framework until that body's demise.

Souls ensnared in such physicality became so blinded by their own selfishness that they cut themselves off from their true spiritual nature and their Creator. Those who were able to remain pure in their descent, the Children of the Law of One, had compassion for the embittered and entrapped Sons of Belial, and they attempted to provide a physical vehicle—*Homo sapiens*—through which souls could again realize their divine nature and regain their true spiritual heritage.

And thus it was that the entranced Cayce explained the physical body of humans and laid the groundwork for the doctrine of reincarnation to be put into effect. At the same time, he established the basis for the continuance of the Atlantean civilization.

The time leading up to the First Destruction saw a period of violent disagreement between the Sons of Belial and the Children of the Law of One over the treatment of the half-human, half-animal "things." While the Sons of Belial enslaved these hapless creatures, making them little better than robots or automatons, the Children of the Law of One taught that these beings were not merely objects, but imprisoned souls that contained the divine spark of the Creator. As such, they were to be helped out of their miserable existence, not kept there for purposes of exploitation.

The Tragic Misuse of the Super Science of the Lost Continent

As noted earlier, Cayce's readings stated that the red race of Atlantis was much more facile in thought than the other racial groups developing on Earth. Before 50,000 B.C., according to his channeled information, the Atlanteans were adept in wireless communications, heavier-than-air flying machines, and even the development of radioactive forces. The "electrical forces" of nature, as Cayce termed them, were harnessed; and the natural gases of the planet's interior were utilized.

Regretfully, the Sons of Belial, already off to a bad start, continued to blacken their record by developing all of these forces of a super science for destructive purposes. It was the pernicious employment of these inventions that caused the First Destruction of Atlantis. The interference with inner-earth gas resources and the misuse of natural electricity caused violent earthquakes and volcanic eruptions in the land.

Following the first breaking up of certain portions of Atlantis, the war continued to rage between the two opposing forces. Scientific and technological advances spiraled. The Atlanteans took a liking to convenience inventions—devices that would lighten their workload.

A more ominous creation was that of the so-called Death Ray or "super-cosmic ray" detailed in a reading given by Cayce in February of 1933. The seer of Virginia Beach spoke also of an infamous crystal that was used by the Sons of Belial to supply Atlantis with power.

According to Cayce, the Atlanteans had also developed television, atomic energy, and numerous chemical and mechanical processes to aid daily life.

In addition to various types of aircraft, Cayce hinted at a means of travel that went beyond machines, rendering them unnecessary. He further suggested that the Atlanteans could travel through elements other than air and could also transmit thoughts through the ether.

After the First Destruction, the population of Atlantis divided itself into two distinct camps. The Sons of Belial strove only for self-gratification and sought to use the instruments of Atlantean super science for material gain, unmindful of the sufferings of others. The Children of the Law of One continued to revere the Creator, respect individual soul growth, and urged caution in the exploitation of the powerful forces they had harnessed.

It is at this point in Cayce's account of Atlantean history that unsettling parallels to the United States begin to appear, parallels that grow increasingly obvious as this nation's technological growth continues to grow virtually unchecked. We can only pray that such comparisons end before our nation replicates the deadly debacle that sealed Atlantis's fate.

In the unconscious trance state, Cayce propounded that even as individual souls reincarnate, so do groups of souls. And even as a single entity incurs a karmic debt, so does a nation. All must pay for deeds perpetrated against others, and they must be repaid in like measure.

The Second Destruction

There is some indication that a shifting of the poles occurred along with the Second Destruction of Atlantis, though this is not clear. It is interesting to note that Cayce saw that large numbers of the great dinosaurs had survived on Atlantis in this period (*circa* 28,000 B.C.), and he even drew a correlation between the use of the powerful Atlantean crystal to rid the planet of these monstrous beasts and the subsequent imbalance of the forces of nature.

The havoc created by this second period of destruction succeeded in breaking up the continent into five major islands, the largest and most advanced of which was Poseidia. A number of Atlanteans managed to flee the landmass as it was splitting asunder and migrate to other areas, but it appeared that the greater portion of the population stoically awaited their destiny.

Violent disagreement still raged over the treatment of the "things." By this time, these misbegotten creatures, some of them carrying physical deformities such as feathered appendages, webbed feet, and other animal-like features, were completely enslaved by the Sons of Belial.

As an additional, insidious aspect of Atlantean culture, the Sons of Belial had discovered cybernetic control of the human brain. They had also cracked the DNA code, thereby enabling them to shape heredity. Such control resting in unethical hands could only result in the creation of more "things."

There are even those metaphysical scholars who will insist that the pig was an Atlantean creation of the Sons of Belial with *Homo sapiens* serving as the base material. Proponents of this theory will point out how similar pork is in substance to human flesh, and the most difficult for us to digest. They will also call attention to the ancient 'Jewish taboo applied to the ingestion of pork, and remind one of the Greek myth of Circe, the enchantress, who turned men into swine.

While such an idea may seem far-fetched, how far removed from such powers are our own scientists who experiment with DNA and genetic manipulation?

In ancient Atlantis, such a manipulation of the laws of heredity proved too great a mockery of the "Creative Forces," as Edgar Cayce always called them. The fatal strain of *hubris* had to be weeded out. The Sons of Belial had become such an effrontery to natural laws that it was the very forces of nature that destroyed them in the end.

The Final Destruction and the Atlantean Records

The Final Destruction was not without warning. The volcanic eruptions and the breaking up of the landmasses occurred over several months, each tremor increasingly more damaging than its predecessor. Such signs were heeded by the Children of the Law of One, several of whom migrated to the Pyrenees, Egypt, the Yucatan, and Og, the present-day Peru.

The imminence of the coming disaster prompted feverish activity among Atlantean record keepers. From time to time, Cayce would inform a client who had come for a psychic reading that he or she had been associated with the preserving of the ancient records of Atlantis and that this work would soon be discovered in modern times.

In my own past-life regressions of clients, I have found mentions of these Atlantean records to surface again and again.

According to Cayce and other metaphysical traditions, there were three principal caches of Atlantean historical records. One set was allegedly left in a temple somewhere in the Yucatan. Another set resides in what has been called the "Hall of Records," a small pyramid in Egypt that has yet to be rediscovered—but which is prophesied to be found before the end of the century. The third set of records was placed in the Poseidian temple of Iltar, which sank with the last remnants of Atlantis.

It is the rising of the temple of Iltar that Cayce indicated would herald the eventual complete reemergence of Atlantis. In 1968, there was some archaeological evidence in support of such a possible occurrence when an ancient sunken "temple" was discovered off the coast of Bimini in the Caribbean Sea. It was in this same area that Cayce had clairvoyantly placed the temple of Iltar.

Atlantean Healings in the Temples of Sacrifice and Beauty

The greatest percentage of Edgar Cayce's Atlantean readings reflect life during, and immediately preceding, the third and final destruction. Much of the information for this period is gleaned from the voluminous Egyptian readings, for Egypt was the principal colony to which the majority of Atlanteans fled.

From a Spontaneous Past-Life Recall Reported to the Author:

My wife and I were scientists on Atlantis who tried to hold segments of the landmass of Poseidia together with the energy from powerful crystals. She was killed during the Final Destruction, and I managed to join a group of others who were headed for Egypt.

I remember as a small child the first time that I heard the name, "Egypt." I actually felt the warmth of the sun on my skin and inhaled the warmish smell of reeds and water.

I have now sensed three lifetimes in Egypt:

A military man who is a great strategist, but who has no feeling for people, the court, or the priesthood. His only interest is to expand and to promote Egypt.

A peasant or slave, whose frustration with life results in self-destruction.

An old man, a refugee from another land, who is learned, but who has contempt for the primitive culture and its people. I expire alone, extremely bitter.

* * *

According to Edgar Cayce, one of the most significant deeds achieved by the Atlanteans before their assimilation into Egyptian culture was the payment of their ages-old debt to the grossly misused "things." In the readings detailing the correction of the creatures' physical deformities, Cayce gave a number of exciting insights into the art of Atlantean healing.

Healing on Atlantis occurred in two temples, the Temple of Sacrifice and the Temple Beautiful. In the first mentioned temple, physical corrections were made—feathered appendages and other animal features were removed. In the second, the soul was purified and creative abilities were developed.

The Atlanteans had discovered the healing properties of color and music. Massage was also used, for the Atlanteans believed that physical manipulation would raise their subjects' own healing powers to their highest spiritual center, whence these powers would spill over into the entire body and promote healing. Undesignated "electrical forces" were used in an unspecified manner to remove unnatural appendages, either surgically, one presumes, or through dematerialization.

The Children of the Law of One did not terminate their obligation to the "things" with the transformation of their misshapen forms into physical perfection. As spiritual beings, the Children of the Law of One knew that their true purpose in life was to fan the fire of the divine spark dwelling within these souls, and they were well aware that a lovely body does not necessarily guarantee a beautiful personality. In the Temple Beautiful, the Atlans, as Cayce called them, awakened the individual soul to its spiritual heritage, then trained the entity in the arts as expressive reminders not to stray from the positive path.

The United States of Atlantis

Edgar Cayce tells us in hundreds of his readings that the vast majority of the American populace has experienced past lives on the lost continent of Atlantis.

If Cayce is correct in his vision that the United States is largely populated by reborn Atlanteans, then it would seem only a very short step to declaring that America herself is the reincarnation of Atlantis. We have certainly been given the opportunities to develop our nation to become the mightiest ever known in recorded history, and we are uncomfortably close to the point that determined the final fate of Atlantis: Shall we use our vast powers for the good of the planet and its people—or shall we use the power for the exploitation of weaker nations and the environmental despoiling of our world?

If the United States is truly Atlantis reincarnated, then we are fast approaching the crucial moment of decision. We have split the atom; we have confused the natural evolution of the planet with pollutants; we have cracked the codes of DNA and can duplicate the building blocks of life in our laboratories; we have developed weapons of destruction so powerful that one thimbleful of deadly bacteria can annihilate all life forms on Earth.

The result of the final choice made by the people of Atlantis is overwhelmingly evident by the complete destruction of their continent. The choice we as citizens of the United States may one day have to make could also make itself known to future generations by the same kind of cataclysmic changes in our continent's landmass.

Cayce's entranced delineation of a nation dying at the hand of its own perverted super science seems to contain definite foreshadowings and forewarnings of our own struggle with a technology that bends and twists moral and ethical considerations. Indeed, as he traveled the Mobius strip of Time, Cayce may have been receiving a vision of the possible future of the United States at the same time that he viewed the past of Atlantis.

The Atlantean Odyssey

To end this chapter on a somewhat more optimistic note, a mediumistic friend once told me that all of humankind's existence on Earth may be but an "Atlantean Odyssey":

The Atlantean Odyssey is now being repeated, and a repetition of events is taking place—but with this one difference: There will be many more of the Creator's children saved from the deluge, because workers in the Light are being given much power and strength in these last days.

Guidance will always be with workers in the Light to help them in any dilemma, any crisis . . . and mark this: There will be much to try human souls in the coming three decades. This is why it is absolutely necessary for all to dedicate all of every twenty-four hours to be tuned-in to God's pathway.

The coming years are such that they will cause many to give up hope. But this is not the way for the Children of Light. They will find that as they become strong in attunement the Red Sea of Death will open for them to pass safely through. Help will come in many diverse ways to all who stand fast in their faith and love in God's path.

Send forth Love and Light to surround Earth daily. Know that, in spite of appearances, all will be well!

CHAPTER TEN

Atlantis's Temple Beautiful Rises Again in Phoenix

In 1973, I spoke with Hugh Lynn Cayce, Edgar Cayce's son, who had been actively involved with his father's work for many years. At that time, the Association for Research and Enlightenment (ARE) had approximately 15,000 members and coordinated more than 1,500 study groups around the world.

"My father was an embarrassment to the medical profession," Hugh Lynn said. "He was not trained. He had no medical background, and he didn't even know the terminology. Yet, in a trance state, he was able to give complete medical diagnoses and prescribe remedies.

"His readings stated that my father's unconscious mind was able to tap the unconscious minds of other people and draw information from them that suggested the correct treatment for them. He insisted that there is a river of thought forms and intelligence at another level of consciousness and that this was the source of his information."

Hugh Lynn told me that his father had believed that we are all psychic.

"But for many people, the manifestation of this ability can be very disturbing, very upsetting; and, in fact, it can even destroy the personality if it runs rampant in the person's life and the individual does not use these abilities constructively," he explained. "If he takes ego trips with it—or begins to fake it—the result can be very destructive to the personality, especially to the personality of young children.

"My son, Dr. Charles Thomas Cayce [the current head of ARE], an experienced child psychologist, is interested in his grandfather's ideas concerning the development of psychic abilities in children. He is in touch with sensitive children all over the land, and he is able to give parents a great deal of help in guiding and developing their children's psychic capacity without upsetting their fragile personalities."

When Edgar Cayce died in 1945 at the age of sixty-seven, he had given nearly 9,000 medical readings while in a state of clairvoyant trance. In addition, the "sleeping prophet" also gave life readings dealing with the vocational, psychological, and human-relations problems of individuals. It was through the life readings that the concepts of reincarnation and the possibility of past lives were introduced. All together, more than 14,000 Cayce readings have been recorded on 200,000 permanent file cards and cross-referenced into 10,000 major subjects.

In 1931, the Association for Research and Enlightenment was chartered in the state of Virginia as a nonprofit organization to conduct scientific and psychical research. Two years after Cayce's death, the Edgar Cayce Foundation was established. The original ARE has become the membership arm of the Cayce programs. The foundation is the custodian of the original Cayce readings and the memorabilia of the great contemporary seer's life and career. Both are headquartered in Virginia Beach, Virginia.

In 1970, the husband-and-wife medical team of Dr. William and Dr. Gladys McGarey established the ARE Clinic in Phoenix, Arizona, and gave new birth to the Temple Beautiful program as it was described in Cayce's Atlantis readings.

In 1986, I collaborated with Stella Andres on the inspirational book, *Stella—One Woman's Victory Over Cancer*. When in 1975, Stella, a Greek–American from New York, had been given the choice of the piecemeal amputation of her legs or the death sentence of lymphosarcoma, she chose to take control of her life and to release the natural healing energies within her own body. Paramount to Stella's recovery was the work of the American mystic Edgar Cayce and the combined efforts of Dr. William McGarey and Dr. Gladys McGarey and their staff at the Association for Research and Enlightenment Clinic, who had recreated the Temple Beautiful of Atlantis in Phoenix, Arizona.

As Dr. Gladys McGarey explained to me, each patient is given a complete physical upon arrival at the clinic and previous records and charts are examined. The staff may or may not try to work out a specific diagnosis, for they consider themselves a therapeutic, rather than a diagnostic, clinic.

The patients work with music and color. They play with colored sheets in the yard as they dance.

"We work with the patients' diet," Dr. Gladys said. "We work with their dreams. They get massages; they get colonics. They get lectures about healings, and they receive a program of laying on of hands. They have an experiential visualization with castor oil packs. They have laboratory work done. They work with biofeedback and visualization. They have an appointment with our psychologist . . . At the completion of the program, they are sent home with a therapeutic regimen to follow.

"We feel that it is very important that the patients understand that the ARE Clinic does not consider itself to be Lourdes. What we feel we are is a place where those who are ill can come to grips with *why* they have the problem and *what* they can do about it."

I also found it fascinating that just as Edgar Cayce had referred to "undesignated electrical forces" that were used in the healing temples on Atlantis, the Temple Beautiful program in Phoenix employs the Electromechanical Therapeutic Apparatus, a device that resembles a bed and which enhances the electromagnetic field in the patient's body.

According to the clinic's explanatory sheet explaining the ETA, "Scientists are discovering that each cell of the body is like a miniature battery that generates and exchanges electricity and magnetism with other cells. When balanced, these energies assist the cells to work better. Weak, pulsating electrical currents are being used to influence cells in ways that can result in speeded-up healing and improved functioning of the mind."

Stella Andres recalled how all of those enrolled in the Temple Beautiful program became closer as the stories of their lives unfolded. Because of the amputation of her leg and the effects of the cancer that afflicted her before her dramatic cure, she had to participate in the color therapy program from her wheelchair.

Later, while receiving a massage, Stella had a vivid past-life flashback and saw herself as a ballerina, "floating across a stage." She could clearly see herself in a pink and gray costume. It was like a movie was projecting somehow on the inner screen of her mind.

Strangely enough, in her present-life experience, Stella is not a ballet enthusiast. "I think I only went once," she said. "And that was before I was married."

Although she had told no one of her inner glimpse of another lifetime as a ballerina, a few days later, a woman her age who was also in the program walked up to her and said:

"We were ballerinas together in another life experience. I had a love-hate relationship with you. You were the head ballerina of a famous dance troupe of which I was a member. Although I loved what you stood for, I hated the type of person you were. You looked down on all of us and expected to be catered to. You were cold and overbearing."

Stella was quite moved by the woman's confirmation of her own past-life recall. In her present-life experience, Stella acknowledged that she may have been catered to when she was very young, but she had grown to be able to handle any responsibility that came her way. That was why, for example, when she had lost her leg, it had become very important to her to be able to take care of herself as quickly as possible.

"I feel that losing my leg in this lifetime was my Karma," Stella said. "Cayce said that Karma is the law of cause and effect regulating one's future life."

I asked Dr. Gladys McGary how she believed a belief in reincarnation might fit into the healing scheme of things.

"I don't think that a belief in reincarnation either 'saves' the person or 'doesn't'," she replied. "I think reincarnation is a logical, rational concept that makes a lot of sense to me. Therefore, reincarnation is helpful to me in understanding people's problems, including their illnesses. If people can accept this concept and look at life as an ongoing process, it seems to me that it is easier for them to accept healing. This is not totally true for everybody, and it is not a necessity."

Barbara Myrick, a biofeedback therapist at the ARE Clinic, became a close friend of Stella Andres and offered both her healing skills and her emotional support to help accomplish the defeat of the deadly cancer. She, too, provided me with a very thoughtful response when I asked what value she placed on reincarnation in the healing process:

"In a **sense**, I think that many illnesses that we encounter may, indeed, be karmic in origin. The way that I see Karma is, you might say, as old thought habits, habits that are involved with guilt or fear or whatever else; and they are habits that are ingrained deep in the subconscious.

"The subconscious is very powerful as far as the body is concerned. If there is a fight between the conscious and subconscious, the subconscious is going to win. It has the power.

"So I think these old karmic patterns are involved in illnesses, but not to the degree that the person has to remember exactly what happened in another lifetime. What they have to learn to unravel is, what is the destructive pattern? How can they change it into a constructive pattern of thought? If, indeed, the old lifetime sheds some insight on that, then it is important. But what *really* is important is learning how to shift that deep inner-thought pattern. And, yes, I think sometimes reincarnational memories or experiences can shed some light on the pattern and allow the person to understand it."

CHAPTER ELEVEN

Viewing Reincarnation Through the Mystic Mind

In the early part of 1970, I was asked by an editor friend at Prentice-Hall if I would write a cover blurb for a book by a new figure on the metaphysical scene, a young psychic-sensitive named Jane Roberts. The book was entitled, *The Seth Material.* And while I wrote an encouraging blurb and was impressed by the woman's clarity of style and her obvious intellect, I could not have predicted then that the entity "Seth" would go on to dictate numerous future volumes and that Jane would become world-famous as a medium.

When she made her own transition to the world of spirit in 1985, I felt, of course, sorrow for the loss of her physical presence and her keen mind, but I knew that she had entered the Great Mystery about which she had written so beautifully. I also recalled a conversation that we had had in the summer of 1975 in which Jane discussed Seth's philosophy of reincarnation.

Central to the spirit entity's teachings is the premise that all reality is created by thought and emotion. Specifically, what a person thinks and feels forms his surrounding reality.

This process of reality-building is not static, however; it is dynamic. Therefore, reality is constantly changing; and it follows that a conscious awareness of this process can change any reality for the better.

In Seth's view, none of us are at the mercy of past events. We cannot blame our parents, our church, our schooling, or any other person or event for making us the way we are. In our ignorance we may have made ourselves unhappy, but with conscious awareness we can make ourselves happy, productive individuals. Because we make our own reality, we can therefore change it.

Seth also taught an extensive theory of personality. It can scarcely be summed up in twenty-five words or less, but it begins by attacking the supposition that the conscious personality that we may call "John" or "Mary" or whoever is one person. John or Mary might be personality manifestations of the same source entity, even though in physical reality they must exist concurrently.

At this point it helps me to understand Seth's

concept of personality by drawing upon the familiar metaphysical theory of the Eternal Now, the Specious Present, or other such terms that refer to a reality freed from the limitations of time. According to such percepts, there is no past, present, and future existing as segmented portions of the time track—all exist as one. Time, therefore, is but an arbitrary system imposed upon our three-dimensional, physical reality. It is a construct that personalities on this plane of existence have created, but they are not really bound to it any more than they are bound to their other creations.

In terms of this concept of the Eternal Now, a single-source self may be manifesting itself in several dimensions at once. Each personality would be operating under the artificial limitations of the plane that it inhabits, and depending upon the individual degrees of development, would be aware or unaware of the various aspects of itself operating on other levels of reality.

Seth's concepts of time and personality intertwine particularly in the theory of reincarnation. According to his unique overview, all lives, or incarnations, on a specific plane are lived simultaneously. Such a concept does not rule out "past" lives, but it does require a different approach to the subject.

An individual facet of a source self, acting according to the laws of his or her particular plane of existence, will either see these lives simultaneously or fit them into that plane's existing time structure. On our Earth plane of reality, because of the division of time into past, present, and future, it is convenient to perceive these various incarnations as neatly separated into these three categories of time.

Seth's belief in mind as the builder expands the concept of personality in a unique way. Since thoughts and emotions create reality, then dreams also have a separate reality. And when we dream of ourselves, we are seeing fragments of our own personality.

Such a concept also extended to an area of reality that Seth called the "probable self."

"According to Seth," Jane told me, "each of us has counterparts in other systems of reality; not identical selves or twins—but other selves who are part of our entity, developing ideas in a different way than we are here in our plane."

These "probable selves" are likened by Seth to distant relatives, who are not as close to us as our reincarnational selves from past lives. To further explain, Seth proposed the metaphor of a tape recorder.

An individual is the master tape with numberless channels. Each channel represents ". . . a portion of the whole self, each existing in a different dimension, yet all a part of the whole self. . . . When the stereophonic channel is turned on, the selves then know their unity. Their various realities merge in the overall perceptions of the whole self . . . Ultimately the inner ego must bring about comprehension on the parts of the simultaneous selves. Each portion of the whole self must become aware of the other parts."

To add further fascination to this concept, Seth suggested that with any given event there are a number of ways to experience it. To the individual ego, it is perceived as a physical event—but each probable way of apprehending the event will be explored by every probable self according to its own time system.

Specifically, if you have a choice among three possible courses of action, you must choose one and then realize it. The other two possibilities will be experienced as well, but not in your physical reality. The probable actions are definitely perceived, however, and Seth says that "it is such experience that makes up the existence of the probable selves just as dream actions make up the experience of the dreaming self." Seth also maintained that all layers of the whole self continually exchange information on an unconscious level.

In such terms, Jane Roberts may have been a physical manifestation of the nonphysical personality Seth; she may even have been one of his probable selves. She could also have been part of a completely other whole self, separate from the whole self of which Seth was a part. Jane constantly sought to understand more completely the relationship she had with Seth and to explain better the nature of their contact.

Our Present Life Paves the Way for Our Next Life

During my many years of friendship with Sybil Leek, the well-known astrologer, Witch, medium, and metaphysical author, we had the opportunity to celebrate two birthdays together—one in Honolulu, the other in Washington D.C.—for our present-life Earth plane entry dates were but a few days apart in February. Although she was a native of Great Britain, she soon became one of America's foremost advocates of enlightened psychism when she moved to United States. Her death in 1982 marked an enormous loss to all of her colleagues and fans who prized her wit, her enthusiasm for life, and her genuine humility.

On one occasion when I complimented her regarding her articulate expression and obvious erudition, she made what I considered at the time to be a rather startling confession.

"In terms of formal education, Brad, I am very uneducated," she said. When I arched a skeptical eyebrow, Sybil added emphatically, "I mean, I am *really* totally uneducated!"

So, I wondered, where did her apparent knowledge come from? Past lives?

"Of course." She smiled. "I believe in reincarnation. As we are in this life, we are paving the way for the next life.

"I have always had my personal proof of reincarnation. As I said, I am totally uneducated. However, there are very few subjects that I cannot tune in on. That may not seem like very practical proof of past lives, but I must have learned something from them. When the need arises, this little 'shutter' of the past clears itself, and I see whatever I need to know very clearly. I see everything absolutely in the right and proper manner.

"I accept completely that death is not the end and that the spirit is indestructible. It would be such a waste if it were not, and it makes more sense. And it is more just.

"We are raised in logic; and what logic is it that a child should die at the age of two when he or she could live three score and ten years? Logic is not the answer."

Sybil paused, as if reflecting on her comments. "I completely accept reincarnation. I could spend the rest of my life trying to *prove* it; but it is there, it always has been, and now let me get on with living. Let me live within the idea that the spirit is going to be indestructible."

Striving to Create Harmony with the Great Mind

Olof Jonsson is the remarkable Swedish-born psychic-sensitive who participated with astronaut Edgar Mitchell in the famous Moon to Earth ESP experiment during the flight of Apollo 14 in 1971. During one occasion when he was spending the weekend with us in our home in Iowa, Olof and I began to discuss the enigma of reincarnation.

Olof said that even before he had left Sweden, he had placed nearly 1,000 into hypnotic trances and led them back to relive what appeared to be their former life experiences.

"One young woman gave names that we were able to trace through old church records," he told me. "She named many members of her family in her former life, and we located old records and deeds to support her apparent memory.

"There were many other cases in which a great number of details of alleged former lives were given by a subject, and we were often able to substantiate a good many of these facts. I have also sent subjects back thousands of years; but even though the historians who were observing agreed that the subjects had the flavor of a past time, there was no way to check a story that goes back so many years."

Olof spoke of the time when he had placed a subject in a very deep-trance state and had moved him from the death experience to a kind of spiritual plateau between lives.

"This entity, in deep trance, said that a physical body is built around a soul and that the relationship continues to develop until the point of physical death. At that time, the soul continues its wanderings in the world of spirit. A span of about 144 years passes before the soul once again takes habitation in a new physical body; and, according to this entity, each soul is reborn an average of twelve times. After the final incarnation, the soul once again becomes a wholly spiritual being."

When the Swedish mystic asked the subject what it was like to live in the world of spirits, he answered that it was wonderful, that he felt so in harmony with the universe.

The entranced subject also informed Olof Jonsson that after the final incarnation, the soul is reunited with its soulmate, the mate that it shared in its first incarnation.

"The soulmate is like one's true 'other half,' and one will be whole and happy after the final incarnation."

Based on his over 1,000 regressions into past lives and his own extraordinary psychic abilities, I asked Olof what he felt happened immediately after the soul left the body in physical death.

"I feel that the soul is translated into a higher dimension. In that dimension, the soul will be *born* as spirit, not as body. On our physical-material plane, we are used to seeing three-dimensional bodies in order to identify a person; but I don't believe that a body structure is necessary in a higher-life condition. I feel that the material plane of existence on which we are living now is but a moment in our *real* lives."

Where does the soul go after physical death?

"The soul leaving the plane of materialism is very much like a voyager leaving the Mainland and venturing out to sea. As time passes, he drifts farther and farther away from the old world. After he has docked in a fascinating new world, he becomes less interested in what he has left behind him and he becomes more concerned about developing the new opportunities before him. At first, the voyager may feel a bit insecure while he is getting to know new friends and so forth; but when he has established a new home, the old Mainland becomes only a part of his memory."

Then why reincarnation? Why do the "voyagers" ever come back to the "Mainland?"

"Not everyone does. I do not believe that everyone reincarnates—or at least not so often.

"I think it is like when the farmer puts seed into the earth; sometimes plants grow . . . and sometimes they don't. I think it may be the same with souls. Not all of them grow properly. And if that is so, then they must be replanted."

Do you believe in Karma?

"If you mean the Divine Laws of Compensation and the Supreme Law of Spiritual Growth, then my answer is, yes. If you mean Karma as some kind of punishment for the soul, then I do not accept it. I do not accept the notion of punishment in the afterlife or in a series of incarnations.

"I believe that we may have to endure certain kinds of sufferings in order to learn important lessons, to clear a situation. But I do not believe that suffering is meant by Divine Intelligence to be a punishment for sins."

At what moment does the soul enter the physical body?

"I believe the soul enters the body when the infant takes its first breath of life upon achieving independence from the mother's womb."

What effect do you think birth control might have on the Wheel of Rebirth?

"I don't think birth control methods have any effect at all on reincarnation. If one misses one train, he simply waits for another."

How might abortion affect reincarnation or Karma?

"I don't think abortion interferes with reincarnation in any way. If you do not buy one automobile, you may soon be interested in another. If you don't get one physical body, you'll get into another."

In view of the spiritual progress of reincarnation, what do you think is the ultimate goal of life?

"I think that what we are working for is not something materialistic. We are striving to achieve Harmony and a reuniting with the Great Mind and its complete knowledge of the Universe."

The Reincarnationist Who Has Given Over 50,000 Past-Life Readings

In addition to being one of the metaphysical world's greatest innovators, Patricia—Rochelle Diegel is an internationally famous reincarnationist who has given over 50,000 individual past-life readings. From their present home in Las Vegas, she and her husband Jon—Terrance Diegel conduct a variety of past-life and awareness seminars, as well as personal readings for a well-satisfied clientele that has sought them out in each of their previous psychic centers in Honolulu, Hawaii; Sedona, Arizona; or Los Angeles, California.

Patricia—Rochelle's interest in reincarnation began with her earliest childhood memory—her own birth.

"I was stillborn. The doctor pronounced me dead as he pulled my tiny body from my mother's birth canal. My body was set aside while the medical team at Harbour Hospital in Detroit concentrated all efforts on my mother.

"Years later, under hypnosis, I could remember seeing the delivery room, and I described it in detail, which my mother verified as correct.

"I remember observing the original soul leaving the body and deciding not to stay there. I—the Real Me, Patricia—Rochelle—was apparently an entity searching for a body.

"I saw a nurse beginning to have an insistent feeling that there was something that she could somehow do to save the dead infant. Acting on this impulse, she fetched a pulmotor and used it to pull the blood from the baby's lungs. She was startled and overjoyed to see the tiny chest lift with its first breath.

"Although it had been thirty minutes from the moment of actual birth to the baby's first breath—and it seemed as though that was a very long time—the Real Me could ascertain that the infant was definitely living and that there was no damage to the brain. Having evaluated the situation and knowing what my destiny on Earth was to be, I decided to inhabit this physical body and to live the life planned for it."

Thus it was under such seemingly unorthodox conditions that Patricia–Rochelle was born. After those thirty minutes of physical death, she feels that she received a jolt of paranormal abilities that continued to grow with her Earth plane body throughout her life.

Her psychism began to express itself in early childhood; and the utilization of such talents into her adult years allowed her to demonstrate a remarkable business and organizational sense. Her stints in many jobs and occupations broadened her compassion for all people, whatever their circumstances might have been; and she feels that she cleared her Karmic slate through a series of marriages, which culminated in her very happy union with Jon–Terrance Diegel.

"I have worked as a private detective, an advertising executive, a real estate salesperson, and an office manager," Patricia–Rochelle told me as she listed her diverse employment background. "I owned total, or parts of, restaurants and other businesses. I even worked in Hollywood as an associate producer and casting director."

Patricia–Rochelle pointed out that her extremely varied background had been of great advantage to her in her psychic work and in her past-life readings.

"I would say that ninety percent of the clients I see come from some type of work or experience with which I have had some experience. It is actually quite exciting to have people sit across from me during a reading and for me to tune in and discover that they are doing something that I have already done. Therefore, I can talk their language."

It was during an extremely busy and hectic part of her life that some friends invited her to attend a meeting of the ARE, the Association for Research and Enlightenment, the organization formed around the medical and past-life readings of the late Edgar Cayce.

"This meeting was the beginning of a new life

for me. I reclaimed the psychicism of my childhood and allowed it truly to mature within me.
My wanderings in and out of jobs, marriages, and
residences ceased. Something really clicked inside
my head. I had come home spiritually."

Patricia—Rochelle underwent more hypnotic regressions and recalled many additional details of
her past lives. The fascination of her spiritual rebirth and the commitment it fired within her
caused her to spend less and less time on her
business enterprises. She began one by one to give
her projects away. She would establish others in
managerial positions, then turn the business over
to them.

"I was finally able to extricate myself completely
from all business concerns. I then moved into the
work of helping people achieve awareness and
personal transformation through the scanning of
their past lives."

As a psychic reader, Patricia—Rochelle told me
that she has the ability to sit across from her clients and sense in her body where they may have
pain.

"I know the places that may be out of alignment
or the places where something is wrong. By giving
my clients this information and then having them
check with a doctor, many of them have been able
to get immediate medical help. Others have had
help occur during the counseling session when

they accepted what I have said about their releasing old Karma."

According to Patricia–Rochelle, a certain color in her clients' auras indicates a heartbreak in their present or past-life experiences.

"Quite frequently there is a pattern of a person sticking his neck out to get his heart broken because of an original cause in a past life. Now in getting to the specific past life with the original cause of his heartbreak and then getting him to release the first broken heart, I must release the chain of heartbreaks down through time and right up to the present incarnation."

Through many years of working as a past-life reader, Patricia–Rochelle has evolved a system of scanning a client's prior-life experiences while wide awake.

"Using this system, I have trained over five hundred people to do their own past-life readings and to read for others.

"Primarily, I am a past-life reader—or a reincarnationist, as I prefer to be called. I call the consultation that I do, an 'Immortality Consultation,' so that I am able to handle the client as an immortal being, using his or her entire time track.

"You can picture a figure eight lying on its side as a continuous strip. Such a figure is called a 'Mobius Strip,' and it is the symbol that I use to show people that they have had more than one incarnation along the time track. They have lived many lifetimes and worn many suits of clothes. The body that they are now using is just one of several older 'suits' that they have worn. And by being aware of these other lives, they can bring the talents, the knowledge, and the abilities they had before into their present body and mind and receive the benefit of all those past lives.

"As for the actual reading itself, I have evolved a system whereby in one hour of time I am able to give clients the information that they need at the present time. I delineate the potentials that they carried into their present life from their past lives. I list the creative, psychic, and other types of knowledge they need to utilize to fulfill the mission for which they came into their present lifetime. I detail the work that they are supposed to do, and I tell them what they have already accomplished spiritually so that they know just what is left for them to do."

Patricia–Rochelle also gives her clients their aura colors, especially the ones pertinent to their present-life expression; and then she answers five questions on their current problems.

"I then proceed to the second part of the reading, which includes my giving them six of their most important past lives and detailing the connection they are experiencing with individuals from those past lives who have come with them in their present lifetime. I usually limit the reading to ten names, so we can cover all of them in a reasonable period of time. If these same entities should appear in the six past lives, fine. If not, I still tell the clients something about these people and where they have been with them in prior lifetimes."

There was a period of time when she felt that it was necessary to give her clients detailed physical descriptions of their past lives, but Patricia–Rochelle has learned that the lengthy recounting of such minutiae did not appear to serve too great a purpose.

"When people attend my past-life workshops, then they themselves are able to get into various detailed aspects of their former-life expressions. I feel that by my offering them a number of successful techniques of past-life recall, including my own method, they will find the one that will suit them best.

"I believe the day has come when all people who are above a certain level of spiritual evolvement are supposed to start knowing about who they were in past lives," Patricia–Rochelle said with great emphasis.

"They should also be able to reach into those lives and pull out the talent, knowledge, and the abilities that they had before—so they can utilize them in their present lifetime. The main reason that I give past-life readings is to help people develop to their full potential."

CHAPTER TWELVE

Reading the Akashic Records, the Divine Consciousness

In 1966, I made the acquaintance of a most remarkable gentleman named Paul Twitchell, who claimed to be able to read the records of souls who had been impressed on the Great Akasha, or Divine Consciousness. Since it had occurred to me that much of what might appear to be past-life recall could be in reality the impressions left by entities from previous generations in some great ethereal reservoir of psychic energy or collective spiritual unconscious, I had already encountered arcane literature that described the Akashic Records. Paul, however, claimed to be able to read these records by projecting his own soul energy to the higher spiritual planes.

At the time we first met, Paul had already

begun conducting seminars on Soul Travel, and he would soon launch his major enterprise, the teachings of Eckankar, on an international scale.

According to Paul, he had learned to read his own soul records while he was projected out of the body in the company of his Tibetan spiritual mentor, Rebazar Tarzs. It was on the fifth plane, the soul plane, that the Tibetan first pointed out Paul's past lives.

"They looked like a fan of playing cards spread over a table," he told me. "They were around my soul like an arc of pictures. These soul embodiments of past lives resembled tiny file cards. Each life had a series of these pictures beginning at birth and passing through all events to death."

When Paul returned to his physical body, he was able to retain what had been shown to him of his past-life experiences in the Akashic soul records. He claimed that nearly anyone who had become proficient at soul travel would be able to read the records of those who requested it.

He stressed, however, that to look at the soul records of another unless given permission to do so was a severe violation of spiritual law.

"The higher one travels on the spiritual ladder, the more he will grant others their own freedom and give less interference to another's state of consciousness," he explained. "As we mount the scale upward, the more ethical we become in our conduct. According to spiritual law, the individual consciousness of a person is his or her home. A spiritual traveler cannot enter unless invited."

I wondered if it wasn't difficult at times not to become involved on some level of consciousness when he saw someone's past- and present-life problems laid out before him.

Paul, a rather short, slim man who dressed always in various shades of blue and seemed always to have a kind of elflike twinkle in his eyes, became serious and told me about the practice of *Vairag,* which he defined as emotional and mental detachment. "Under no circumstances must those who read these records become involved in the problems of others unless he is specifically asked to assist."

According to Paul, the Great Akasha has a record of the divine laws of debt (Karma) and duty (Dharma). Just as the Christian gospels state ". . . whatsoever a man soweth, that shall he also reap," so, insisted Twitchell, do the psychic forces that emanate from us always come full circle and return to us.

"Good readers of the Akashic Records will give their clients the events of certain past lives that are affecting them today in their present lives," he explained. "It depends upon the judgment of the Akashic readers to give whatever lives and whatever events they think are causing the present problems and to offer suggestions on how to resolve them."

Paul pointed out that too many people wanted to hear readings that would help them to build up their ego. "They want me to tell them that they have been some important person in history. Such an attitude is self-defeating, for a reading on past incarnations should be a therapy, a cleansing, an understanding of one's past lives. If it isn't, then it doesn't do much good."

A Bachelor Pays for his Past-Life Selfishness

Twitchell told me of his recent reading of the Akashic Records for a middle-aged bachelor.

"He interrupted me and demanded that I give him a vivid account of his sexual adventures in his past lives. Naturally, I declined."

Through an examination of the Akashic Records, Twitchell learned that the bachelor was, in his present life, attached to his mother's apron strings. She controlled the estate that the man would one day inherit; and to please her own selfish whims, she would not permit him to marry.

"This all proved out in his past lives. There had been a time in a prior-life experience when he had controlled her in a similar manner—and now he was paying for his previous selfishness."

Obsessed with Aunt Sally

Paul said that on many occasions clients might have residual scraps of past-life memories that influence them to act in strange ways in their present incarnations.

"I had one female client, who, as a child, would not allow anyone to call her by any other name than Sally, which was not her name at all. Sally had been the name of an aunt who had died just before the child was born.

"The aunt's death was doubly tragic; for not only did she die a very young woman, but she died only a few days before she was to have been married. The young girl grew up with all the characteristics of her aunt Sally. She seemed obsessed with the idea of getting married. Finally, at eighteen, she was wed to a responsible man, who, in turn, appeared to have similar characteristics to the man whom her aunt Sally would have married had she lived. I suppose she might even have married her aunt Sally's fiancé if that poor man had not himself met with a fatal accident after the death of the original Sally."

Paying Off the Karma of Pride and Bad Temper

Paul Twitchell gave an intriguing reading for a Mrs. Lillian Hart of Mohawk, New York.

"From your first incarnation," he told her, "your

pride has been great; but you have been coura-

pride has been great; but you have been coura-geous to the point of sometimes losing your life. Yet your temper has been too strong, forceful, and at times, unpleasant. It has been this quality that has hurt your health so much even in this life. This is one of the threads of Karma that has come down into this present time.

As an aside, he told the woman: "Please don't think that Karma is all bad, for it isn't. The word Karma is used for the whole law of retribution—or cause and effect. It is a countercheck, a balance between the good and the bad of one's conduct and experiences on Earth.

"In your case, you are now paying for this Karma with your bad health and afflictions. One must either go through these experiences or learn to avoid them. . . . Since it is only experiences that make us aware of the Ultimate Kingdom of God, then it is these experiences that purify us and make us eligible to enter into the kingdom again."

According to Paul Twitchell's reading of the Akashic Records, Lillian Hart was controlled by pride during her first incarnation in the Temple of the Bull on Crete. As a male poet under one of the early Shang rulers in China, the soul entity of Lillian Hart stubbornly fought the emperor for peasant reforms.

As the wife of a wine merchant in Jerusalem, Lillian Hart became a fanatical follower of the teacher Jesus of Nazareth.

But Lillian Hart's most significant early incarnations occurred during the persecution of the Christians under Nero. Because she adamantly refused to betray the hiding place of her fellow Christians, her eyes were put out with hot irons.

Paul showed me Lillian Hart's letter in response to his Akashic reading for her:

"My Akashic record received and read many times with great interest and increased understanding of many things.

"I was thrilled to read about my life in the time of Jesus, for I have had vibrations in that respect. . . .

"I have a question about my eyes. . . . You say this is mainly the problem with my eyes today. No doubt you mean the blindness. Or do you mean the pain also? During most of this life I have suffered aching and distress in my eyeballs with frequent spells of very severe pain, like something was boring into my eyes, unbearable at times. . . .

"I was very pleased when you said that I was a fine pianist in France . . . I have always had a strong desire for piano music in this life. . . ."

To Lillian Hart's husband, Paul wrote: "You have a love that has sustained you for centuries. You should never part from this love . . . it has wrapped a protective aura around both of you throughout the centuries, whether you were husband and wife, friends, relatives, or parent and child. . . . You have been a good combination with your wife in this life and in past incarnations, especially the ones whom I have named. You were the husband in the most recent one, the Englishman that she married. Often you were the wife. But you have always been together—and that is the most important part of your relationship."

Rising Above the Time Track to Read the Akashic Records

To read the Akashic Records, Paul Twitchell said that he must project himself via his soul body so that he might rise above the time track and study the lives of whomever had requested a reading.

"It doesn't make any difference where the clients might be—Australia or the Arctic Circle," he told me. "Once I rise above the time track in my soul body, I can read the lives of anyone. I must look at the lives of my clients, spread out like a fan of hundreds of playing cards. And I must look at the millions of little file cards, which are memories of past lives, in order to select what I believe to be most important to my clients and the problems that they are facing today. Next, it is up to me to make suggestions about how they might go about dissolving the karmic debts that they have accumulated."

Revealing a Purposeful Earth Mission

Brian Seabrook of Phoenix is a psychic-sensitive who also claims the ability of reading the Akashic Records for his clientele. I first met Brian in the early 1970s, and I have always considered him to be a very sincere and thoughtful person, as well as a psychic of great integrity. Our mutual friend, journalist Alan Weisman, once described Brian as someone who might remind you more of a "candy-giving uncle than a spiritual medium," whose tone is "even-keeled and intentionally undramatic."

Once when we were both featured speakers at a past-lives conference and had a few hours to spend in semileisure, I took advantage of the lull between lectures to discuss reincarnation and the Akashic Records with Brian.

As a psychic sensitive and as a reader of the Akashic Records, what is it that people seem to most want to learn from you?
People are interested in reincarnation to gain some glimpse of their sense of unease and to learn why they feel so unfulfilled and out of harmony with the universe.

The clients that I meet also feel that there is a mission to which they should be responding. They want to dedicate themselves to something meaningful, purposeful, and transcendent.

Such feelings are not confined to any single age group or any single social category. It is a common thread running throughout America.

Are you able to reach any conclusions about life directions? Are there things that many of your clients see in common as to their life purpose?

Perhaps the most striking common characteristic is the surprise that many people evidence as they approach a major turning point in life. The death of a loved one, a divorce, or a change of occupations are obvious turning points; but evidently there are other, more subtle, inner changes of values, priorities, lifestyles, and psychological needs that prompt an investigation of past-life influences.

In other words, many people reach a point in their self-awareness when they ask, "Is this all there is?"

Or, to put it yet another way, many men and women have set their lives into molds, assuming that they have everything "figured out," only to find that their assumptions are outmoded. They have reached a different state of self-sensitivity. Their personal world has changed, and they must adapt. And as they adjust to new circumstances, new levels of awareness, they make new discoveries about their inner world.

*   *   *

And past-life recall may be one of those new discoveries in a person's inner world?

I think what we are seeing is a discovery of a higher selfhood, a more universal, less restricted personal identity. Such a discovery may cause uncertainty and doubt at first, of course. But a tolerance for ambiguity is evidently one of the signs of personal growth and evidence that a more fulfilling life is coming into being.

The stage of higher selfhood requires an inquiring mind, a nonjudgmental, open attitude toward life, a faith that there is something to be gained and a new potential to be realized, lived, and enjoyed.

Reincarnation answers the quandary for many people; it erases the unease, the lack of purpose. It replaces those uncomfortable feelings with new adventure, hope, and above all, places the individual in touch with aspects of his or her own personality and being that may have been hidden.

Reincarnation also brings about the understanding that all humankind is alike in many ways—we all sense the same joys, fears, hopes, and aspirations through many lifetimes.

Since reincarnation deals with the history of the soul, how have you seen your clients deal with the attitude of more traditional religionists on the subject of past lives?

Strangely enough, most people do not see an

investigation of reincarnation as having anything to do with their traditional religious affiliation—a fact that might surprise most clergy.

I think this is because once a person has grown into a feeling of universal truth, he or she may view traditional church concepts as simply a form of truth or a window on some aspects of life, and not as rigid, dogmatic, ironclad doctrines.

Seekers of truth will simply ignore those theological constructs that are not relevant to their self-discovery. Students of reincarnation may not be antireligious, but they are probably willing to bypass the incongruities of organized religion in favor of an ever-changing spirituality.

However, some spiritual seekers are able to maintain an active religious affiliation that they now see in a more symbolic light. Religion, to them, may have become more like an art form than a specific science.

Students of reincarnation are open to new ideas, are willing to sacrifice self-concepts for a higher, more satisfying diversity of experience. While a crisis situation may have prompted the original query into the subject, steady balance soon emerges and most often new paranormal insights are drawn.

In your view of past lives, do you believe that a soul may have incarnations in worlds or dimensions other than Earth?

Many people whom I have counseled about their past lives have felt that the Earth plane is not where reality is. They have felt uncomfortable with the entire game of Earth life. They talk of another plane in the universe that seems more like home.

We may not be outcasts sent to Earth, as some have theorized. We may be missionaries placed here to seed a new consciousness for humankind.

Many people sense lives, then, on other planets, at other places in the universe. They have no difficulty feeling an extradimensional life, or communicating with unseen forces and entities.

CHAPTER THIRTEEN

Past-Lives Therapy Heals a Volatile Relationship

Ramón Stevens of Ojai, California, provided me with a most interesting account of how a past-lives regression was able to resolve a volatile situation between him and a young friend.

"My hope in sharing this information is that people will realize that relationships fraught with inexplicable emotions and volatile energy might well have been recast from other lifetimes and that past-life therapy can be of immeasurable value in understanding the origin of such otherwise baffling relationships," he said. "For Paul and me, certainly, the result has been greater clarity about why we are here, why we know each other, and how we can best make use of our time together.

"Today, Paul and I share a warm friendship enriched by our knowledge of the karmic ties between us. Ours is clearly a case where the information gained through past-life hypnosis brought an end to a period of confusion."

The Past-Life Narrative of Ramón Stevens

In my early twenties I spent a summer working at a YMCA camp in the Berkshire Mountains of Massachusetts. One day early in the season, before camp opened, a fellow staff member arrived accompanied by his young son. Paul was a handsome and well-mannered towhead, though shy and quiet. We met on his twelfth birthday, and he remembers me sitting beside him at dinner, cracking jokes to put him at ease in a sea of adult company.

Three years later I began graduate school in New York City, and Paul visited occasionally to see me and other friends. During one visit I was watching Paul from across the room when I suddenly felt a surge of warm, loving energy streaming from him to me, enveloping my body. I had felt an intense though inexplicable closeness with Paul for some time; and as he left, I said, "I have a feeling we're going to be very close friends someday."

Our relationship developed two striking qualities. First, we shared a powerful, though nonsexual, affection of an intensity rare in our society, given the strictures against affection between men. We slept in the same bed, gave each other backrubs, fell asleep in each other's arms. Whenever we were together we felt compelled to be in direct physical contact, whether playing footsie under the table or holding hands while walking down the street. After spending a night with Paul, I awoke suffused with a peacefulness I had never known.

The second unusual quality to our relationship was a dynamic attraction-and-repulsion between us. While I loved Paul and loved being with him, at times a revulsion, anger, or enmity would inexplicably well up from inside; at these times I would have to keep my distance until the negative emotions subsided. Nothing Paul said or did triggered such inexplicable black moods; they gripped me without apparent cause.

Paul and I attended a camp reunion one autumn. At night we were using a Ouija board with some friends when Paul and I were ordered by the "spirit" commanding the board to go down to the lakeside docks. We arrived at the docks, feeling somewhat foolish, and were just about to turn back when at the same instant we both heard an imperious command booming in our heads: "Hug him!"

Wordlessly we embraced as a high-voltage flow of electricity crackled between us. For most of an hour we stood locked together, riveted by the churning flow of supercharged energy streaming between our chests.

By this time it was apparent that something beyond our present-day selves, some extraordinary influence, was affecting us. One night Paul and I set a Ouija board between us and asked for answers to the puzzle of our relationship. In rapid staccato bursts the pointer spelled out, "RAMÓN TAKE PAUL TO SALEM BECAUSE HE HAS TO LEARN ABOUT HIS PAST."

I felt myself slipping into a drowsy, trancelike state. Paul and the room faded from awareness. Suddenly I "remembered" a scene with Paul and me, in another place and time, in the woods beside a village. I managed to mumble, "In the woods . . ." and felt a sudden sharp blow to my abdomen.

A seething, though invisible, mob surrounded me, raining blow after blow as I writhed and screamed. I knew Paul was present in the scene, but could not find him.

Far in the distance, as through miles of ocean, I could hear Paul's soothing words, anchoring me to present-day reality.

Now determined to get to the bottom of what had become an increasingly volatile and bizarre relationship, I attended a past-life workshop conducted by New York hypnotherapist Shala Mattingly. One of the past-life sequences that emerged was of a preacher in an early New England town. I had sharp features, a piercing gaze, and jet black hair. I was standing at the pulpit, thundering with vehement passion and fervor while the congregation grew angry. As the vision faded, I saw myself fleeing the building while an angry mob followed.

Intrigued by the possible connection between this past-life memory and the Ouija board experience, I arranged a private session with Shala. Under her skillful questioning, a detailed story spilled out.

I saw myself as a seventeenth-century New England minister in Salem who, though devoted to his wife, could not resist having an affair with a young, attractive widow new to the town. After our affair was discovered by the townspeople, the minister defended himself at the pulpit—his self-righteous defense of free love falling on very deaf Puritanical ears—and was chased from the church into the woods. There he was pummeled by a flurry of sticks and stones.

When they dragged the widow up, she faced a stark choice: she could renounce her lover and thereby spare her children lifelong shame, or she could admit her complicity and be branded for life. As a mother her first loyalty was to her children: she joined in the frenzied beating and delivered the final, fatal blow.

Ramón: For her children's sake she's doing it. . . . She's yelling, yelling names at me. Saying that I have fouled her, defiled her, taken her out of her place in heaven out of my own base lust. And now . . . the others are following suit . . . they see her throwing the rock. . . .

Shala: Stay calm and relaxed. View it merely as an observer without pain or emotion.

Ramón: They're throwing rocks, but there are only so many rocks on the ground. They get sticks. It's a horrible thing . . . there's something explosive . . . They've lost their minds.

I'm lying down now, and they've all stopped, except for her. They're just letting her finish it. . . . She's just beating me to death . . . with a crazy look on her face.

Our eyes meet, and there's just a flicker of sadness . . . because she knows she's lying. But she has to do it for her children . . . she looks at me as if to say, "I'm sorry, but I have to. I'm sorry." When she lifts her head so the crowd can see her face, she puts back on that crazed look of betrayal. But when she looks down at me, it's just love.

She wants to stop now . . . she doesn't want to finish it . . . But they tell her it's the only way she can get back her place in heaven. (Ramón's head suddenly jerks violently to the right.) Oh! Right here (he points to his left temple). That was it.

Shala: That was the end?

Ramón: [Deep breathing] Now I'm above her. I'm just looking down.

Shala: You've crossed over into spirit.

Ramón: She drops the stick. The crowd leads her away. My wife comes up ... she falls to her knees ... and puts her head on my chest. (He begins to weep and asks for a tissue to wipe away his tears.)

Shala: Do you stay near your body for very long?

Ramón: No, I can't stand it. I can't stand to see my wife cry.

Shala: Do you start to withdraw?

Ramón: I went back down beside my wife. I tried somehow to merge with her, to let her know I was still there and care about her; but she doesn't hear me.

Shala: Can you sense any color or sounds as you move on in spirit now?

Ramón: It's just like clouds, white clouds at first. I'm alone.

Shala: You're not aware of any other entities around you?

Ramón: Now I'm coming to some ... They're greater than I am, somehow; I don't mean physically, I mean with their knowledge, their experience. There's three of them. Their bodies are like white masses, kind of shiny and smooth, but they have human faces so that I'm not scared and so I know that it's all right to be with them.

Shala: And are they communicating anything in particular to you at this time?

Ramón: They surround me and . . . we just merge. It's like I'm being implanted with a huge store of knowledge that's passing from them into me.

Shala then led me to the level of the superconscious mind, where I witnessed the planning sessions in which, under the counsel of spirit guides, the minister's and widow's souls "set up" future lifetimes in which their deep karmic bond could be released. I immediately understood the previously inexplicable features of my relationship with Paul:

Ramón: The affection that we share is a recreation of making love. It was such a powerful thing for me in that lifetime, to be with a free spirit who let herself enjoy it. The thing is, we're both male this time and there's a reason for that.

Shala: What is the reason?

Ramón: We're not permitted to have sex this lifetime, therefore we chose the same sex as a way of ensuring that.

Shala then "progressed" me far into the future of this lifetime, to a point where Paul and I could fully heal the karmic bond between us.

I beheld a sick boy before me and, with Paul

holding me tightly, found I could heal a tumor inside the boy's body by channeling the intense loving energy generated between Paul and me. The point is that our karmic bond would not be healed with an eye-for-an-eye act of vengeance, but by blending our energies into a bond of such intense healing and love that the negativity would be neutralized. Whether this vision is actual prediction or simply a metaphor is immaterial. The point is that Karma is not healed through retribution or punishment, but by "victim" and "perpetrator" sharing healing, loving energy of an intensity equal to the original harmful act.

Ten years have passed since the session with Shala, and my relationship with Paul has settled into a much more stable and gratifying friendship, no longer rocked by volatile energies and inexplicable dark moods. We see each other once or twice a year to share a skiing or backpacking adventure.

It amuses us that some consider it a "burden" to carry karmic debts created by past incarnational selves; we feel blessed and fortunate to carry such a bond, for it enriches the depth of love we feel for each other, and gives an *importance* to our time together. We know we are much more than our present-day selves, and that the love we share ripples through the centuries to heal a bond born of passion, murder, and betrayal.

In his article, "The New Age, the Mythic, and

Legitimization of Regression/Releasement Therapy" in The *Journal of Regression Therapy,* Volume VII, Number 1, December 1993, Dr. Carl Silver writes that the "cutting edge of all direct experience, of access to inner wisdom and its mythical expression, is nonlinear and nonintellectual." If the spiritual seeker and his or her guide are to unfold an optimum healing experience, Dr. Silver states, "they must spend a great deal of time together in a nonlinear state of mind."

This is, by definition, an altered state of consciousness, a key ingredient for healing of any kind. Altered states are ordinary and quite normal. Later, so-called left-brain linear thought processes are utilized in order to integrate prior healing experiences. . . . Inspection of societies always reveals belief systems with attendant mythologies, all of which grow out of primarily right-brain non-linear thought processes that are then collated and codified into systematized internal law and practice by primarily left-brain thought processes. As we can see, both left and right are ultimately needed in a balanced way. . . .

Dr. Silver advises us that the key to the true healing process lies not in pondering the truth of mythic figures and events, but ". . . in the willingness to believe that 'Spirit' or 'God' or 'Creative

Force' is in and behind everything that manifests, and that It brings us the laws that guide us in how to conduct our lives.

"It means respectfully acknowledging right-brain's assertion that there is a force from which we ourselves come that knows everything, from which we learn through inspiration, and to which we yearn to return."

... re is art behind everything that maddens, and that is brings us the law, that made us to law to control our lives.

The name, especially, acknowledging of the brain's assertion that there is a force from which we can draw force that knows everything from which we learn people ourselves, force which we learn to follow.

CHAPTER FOURTEEN

We have Lived and Loved Before

In the mid-1970s, a correspondent of mine named Roy went camping with his family in the North Cascades of Washington state. Roy, a born-again Christian, was appreciating the beauty of nature while he was canoeing across Baker Lake with his son. He remembers that he was feeling very God-connected and that he gave thanks for the majestic beauty of the Pacific Northwest.

"Little did I know that I was about to enter a kind of spiritual 'twilight zone,'" Roy informed me. "Suddenly without any warning, strange memories flooded my mind. I looked up at the mountains and realized that somehow I knew them like the back of my hand.

"Then I remembered being in the middle of the

same lake in a similar canoe—but with a different body!"

Dimly aware that he seemed to be recalling a prior-life experience, Roy felt a great conflict with his religious beliefs. He tried to pray the past-life memories away. . . .

"But they were *real*! I tried to escape them by leaving the lake with my son as quickly as possible, but memories continued to flood my mind, even weeks later."

Roy decided to use charismatic prayers and the blood of Jesus Christ to ask God for an answer to the unwelcome memories.

"God's answer was to show me a crystal-clear memory of the woman who I loved in that life!"

Discovering Jacob and Isabel

After reading a number of Edgar Cayce books on reincarnation, Roy decided to visit a hypnotherapist in order to explore more details of an ostensible past life through the process of regression.

"Here's what came: I was a French Canadian fur trapper named Jacob. I had crossed the continent and ended up in the Pacific Northwest. My traveling partner, Pierre, and I established temporary residence with a tribe of Native Americans near Puget Sound.

"I/Jacob saved the life of the chief. With the bond of trust now proven, the chief entrusted me with his adopted daughter, Isabel, a beautiful teenager with dark eyes and long, black hair. Although she could easily pass for an Indian, her real father was a white man, who was an abusive alcoholic. The chief asked me to take her with me into the mountains and to hide her in the wilderness before her father came looking for her.

"Although Pierre knew my destination, he did not follow us into the mountains. He had decided to go his own way, as he seemed to be born under a wandering star.

"Isabel and I made temporary camp at the northeast end of what is today called Baker Lake in the North Cascades of Washington. We fell in love, and I swore to protect her all of my life.

"After a number of months of hiding, it became necessary for me to move Isabel to a new location. I chose a remote beach on the shores of Puget Sound, and we eventually built a cabin. My old partner Pierre occasionally visited us, and he was one of the few visitors we had.

"Our relationship was beautiful beyond words, and our stillborn child was our only real sorrow.

"And then, suddenly, I/Jacob died at the jaws and paws of a bear.

"Isabel became so lonely at the loss of her great love, that she willed herself to die within a year.

"In that lifetime, neither Isabel nor Jacob lived to be thirty."

*   *   *

Roy shared these memories with a small circle of trusted friends, and he often wondered if the soul of "Isabel" had also returned in the present time period. If she had—and if he were ever to meet her—would he be able to recognize her?

Or, he kept testing himself, was this all just some incredible fantasy?

Rejoining the Eternal Circle of Life and Love

In August 1981, Roy found himself rejoining a remarkable circle of love and life.

"I was divorced at that time, and I had met an attractive woman named Susie at church. For some reason, both of us seemed to keep trying to avoid each other, but we just kept running into each other, anyway. When we discovered that we both liked to play bridge, our love of the game prevailed—and we ended up as partners one might.

"After an evening of cards, I started discussing my strange experience of seeming to remember a past life as a fur trapper—and Susie interrupted me and began to describe the cabin that Isabel and I had shared. I refused to believe my ears, and I started trying to explain it away.

"Susie then said, 'We had a stillborn son!' "

Roy recalled that all he could manage at that point was to mumble an "ohmygod."

Then he gazed deeply into Susie's eyes and recognized the soul of Isabel.

"Her mentioning of the stillborn child that we had had gave me unavoidable proof of our life together. Two days later, she produced a two-year-old journal that she had kept concerning her memories of Jacob and Isabel. We have been together ever since."

As Roy pointed out, what makes their story so remarkable is that each of them had known about "Jacob and Isabel" years before they reconnected in their present-life experience.

Susie, in her correspondence to me, stated that she had believed in reincarnation since she was twelve years old.

After her divorce became final in 1977, she was totally content to play the role of a single parent and career woman. She had decided that there was no longer any time in her life for men except as friends, and she developed a reputation as "always the women's-lib advocate."

Two years later, while meditating in her personal sanctuary, Susie received such a profound visionary experience that upon her return to full wakefulness she wrote it all down.

"The man in my meditation put his arms around me and told me his name was Jacob. He said that we had been together in the late 1700s in the Puget Sound area and that he was a fur trapper who had migrated down from Canada. After telling me a number of details about that lifetime, he said that we belonged together in this time also and that he would be coming to find me soon, but he had to tie up some loose ends first."

Susie shared her journal with a couple of close friends, who suggested that she keep her eyes open for this soulmate. But after about a year, she decided that she had imagined the whole episode, filed her journal away, and "tucked the experience" into the back of her mind.

In August 1981, completely unaware that her life was about to undergo radical change, she made an "appointment" for a bridge game with a man she had met at church. Mentally, she didn't even acknowledge the evening as a date, and she had even arranged for them to drive separate cars and to meet at the host's home.

After the game, she surprised Roy by asking him out for a drink and they began to discuss their various personal beliefs. Eventually, late in the evening, he shared the story of his alleged past life as the Canadian fur trapper who had settled in the Pacific Northwest.

Susie was speechless. "He didn't notice my eyes bulging or my jaw dropping as he continued to tell me about his memories of Jacob, who was born in France but was forced to flee when his parents were killed by revolutionaries."

When Roy got to the part about the Northwest, she stopped him and began asking questions:

"You had a cabin on the water?"

"Yes."

"With one small window facing east?"

"Yes."

"And your wife had a stillborn child?"

"Oh, my God!"

Roy and Susie sat staring at each other. Then they hugged each other and cried.

They sat in Roy's car and talked until 4:00 A.M.

Two weeks later, they took the weekend off and drove the ninety or so miles to Baker Lake, where Roy had first had the flashbacks of his life as Jacob.

Nothing seemed right until they stopped at the mouth of a small stream that fed the lake. They got out of the car, walked down to the shore, and felt that they were very close to finding some of the answers for which they searched.

Roy said that he wanted to walk down the river a little way to "check his traps." Susie decided to stay and get in touch with some of the feelings that she was experiencing.

"I was in for another surprise," she said. "The moment that Roy was out of my sight, I panicked and began to shake and cry. I wanted to call out to him to come back, but I was too afraid to make any noise. This was all so strange to me. As a dedicated feminist, it was just not my style to stand by a river in broad daylight and cry for my man to come back and protect me."

That night, Roy, who had become a hypnotherapist in the years since he, as a born-again Christian, had first experienced those puzzling past-life memories, regressed Susie to the late 1700s in the Pacific Northwest.

She was uncertain of her name in that life, but they settled on "Isabelle" as the closest about which she felt right. The story that unfolded began when she was a child of seven and lived somewhere with her parents in the eastern United States. After her mother died, her father, who was physically, sexually, and emotionally abusive, hauled her across the wilderness with a small group of men. Isabelle was terrified of her father, but she had no choice.

"Eventually, when I was around nine and we were finally out west, an Indian chief my father knew either bought me, stole me, or negotiated for me. All I remember is that I was given to the chief and my father left the area. The chief adopted me, and since I had long black braids and brown eyes, I fit right into the tribe and had a loving home once again.

"When I was around twelve, there were rumors that my father was back in the area and planned to reclaim me and take me away. To keep me safely away from harm, the chief asked Jacob, his dear friend, to take me into the wilderness to hide me until the danger had passed.

"We went to a cabin on a lake in the Cascade Mountains, where Jacob gave me strict instructions *never* to let him out of my sight or to make loud noises that might call attention to us. That was where my panic had come from when Roy was out of sight.

"My father never found me. Jacob and I lived on in the cabin for about another seven years and fell deeply in love. He was my whole life. When he was killed by a bear behind the cabin, my life was over. I refused to leave the cabin where we had been so happy, and I died soon afterward."

At the time that Roy and Susie wrote to me in 1988, they had been married for five years.

"We've been through some tough times that I believe would have broken a couple who didn't have our bonds," Susie said. "At one point during a long, drawn-out crisis, we considered splitting up—simply because it would have been easier. We didn't choose the easy way. Instead, we reaffirmed our commitment that our relationship is the most important factor in our lives. After all, when you've been together a few hundred years, current challenges attain a different perspective!"

Karmic Debts Can Complicate the Best of Relationships

Throughout the ages, there have been few tales more romantic than those that tell of reincarnated lovers who have once again managed to find each other over the span of centuries.

However, too many of these reunited lovers have entered a relationship—marital or otherwise—without being consciously aware of their previous-life times and their karmic debts to one another. These love partners may experience personal anguish and discover that their lives have become miserably complicated.

Sadly, because they are looking for answers to their incompatibility in their present lives only, they may spend both countless hours and dollars with a regiment of marriage counselors, psychiatrists, psychologists, and clergy without ever gaining a clue to their dysfunctional relationship.

When I was conducting individual regression sessions, it seemed as though they came to me in an endless line from all over the United States—men and women with marital maladjustments, emotional entanglements, and sexual traumas. Through relaxation techniques and past-life regressions, I was able to help these troubled people discover that the origins of many of these difficulties appeared to lie in their previous-life experiences. These clients were able to see for themselves that not only have they lived before, they may have loved before in prior-life relationships.

And as I and numerous past-life therapists have stressed throughout this book, whether such reincarnational recalls are fantasies or actual past lives coming forth as memories, many men and women have obtained definite and profound release of present-life phobias by reliving the origin of the trauma in some alleged former existence. As has been frequently stated before in these pages, a belief in reincarnation is not necessary for the subject to experience a benefit from the cathartic vision or fantasy.

After 150 Years, Her Seaman Had Finally Come Home

When Esther came to me, she was suffering from a general insecurity about her marriage with Carl. She felt that her husband was sometimes coldly aloof and often gave the impression that he was complete in and of himself without her.

Through regression, I learned that the two had shared a past life in New Bedford, Massachusetts, *circa* 1850. In that lifetime, Esther had fallen in love with the soul that was Carl, who, in that prior-life experience, had been a young seafaring man. Although he was amorous enough when he was home, he always answered the call of the sea and left the entity who was now Esther waiting on the dock.

After I had conducted a lengthy regression with both of them, their present marriage became more secure when Esther was helped to realize that, in this lifetime, Carl had come home to her arms to stay. Carl, on the other hand, had to recognize that he needed to be more expressive in his love for his wife and to share his inner feelings, rather than repressing them.

The Tormented Self-Condemnation of a Workaholic

Megan had large, dark circles under her eyes as she sobbed out her story to me. She was seriously considering divorce because Charles was obsessed with his work to the point of almost total neglect of their children. He had become a total workaholic who begrudgingly took time off only for holidays and birthday observances.

Through a very deep regression, Megan relived a life of terrible poverty and famine in which she had also been married to the soul expression who was now Charles. In anguish, she saw them burying five of their eight children, as one by one they starved to death. Once again, she heard her past-life husband's tormented self-condemnation as he cursed himself for being a poor provider.

Megan returned to her marriage suffused with a greater understanding of Charles's obsession for his work and with a plan of how she might alleviate the sense of guilt that he had carried with him from that previous lifetime of awful misery.

She Had No Desire to be Another Baby Factory

It was easy to understand Mike's frustration when he and his attractive wife Kim came to me for a past-life exploration. Tearfully, Kim admitted that even though she loved her husband she simply could not enjoy having sex with him.

After an in-depth regression, it was discovered that the two had been previously united in a rather primitive relationship in the Middle East of several hundred years ago. The soul-entity that was now Mike had had several wives and had treated them all as mere baby factories. In that lifetime, Mike had only been interested in adding to his prestige and wealth by fathering more sons to tend to his flocks. He had impregnated the soul that was now Kim a total of nine times in that prior-life experience—and he had murdered three girl babies before her anguished eyes.

The karmic-carryover had left the present-life Kim reluctant to engage in intercourse with Mike for fear of his making her assume her brood-mare status. Thankfully, the regression helped her to realize that she and Mike had been given the opportunity to love again in more enlightened times.

Ben Was Afraid of Losing Wendy Once Again

Ben Kranzler spoke honestly to Dick Sutphen about what was troubling him. "I have to admit that I feel threatened. Wendy wants to get out into the world more. She wants the freedom to come and go as she pleases. I even get a knot in my stomach when I see her reading *Cosmopolitan*. Maybe I worry about being inadequate? I just wish that she could be happy staying home with the kids, like she used to be."

Ben and his wife Wendy, both in their midthirties, had come to Sutphen for help in their troubled marriage.

"What kind of relationship do you desire, Wendy?" Sutphen asked.

Her quick response carried the tone of some underlying hostility. "I'd just like to be free to be me. I don't want a sexually open relationship, but neither do I want to have to answer for every minute of my day—or get into a fight with Ben because I have an innocent drink with a male friend. We used to have a fine sex life; but for the last several months, our constant hassles have caused it to go downhill."

Ben nodded silently in agreement.

Sutphen knew that the couple had been participants in one of his five-day past-life seminars. "You know that I am not a marriage counselor," he reminded them. "And you've already heard my spiel about man/woman relationships from a metaphysical perspective."

"Yeah," Ben answered wryly. "And you seem to agree with Wendy's present directions."

"Now wait," Sutphen cautioned. "This isn't a matter of taking sides. I do believe in a relationship of freedom and trust between two people, because I've seen it work better that way. But, Ben, you are experiencing very real anxieties. Possibly, if you could more fully understand them, you could begin to rise above them. We all think we have problems; yet it really isn't the problem that concerns us—it is the effect of that problem. That is, how we allow it to affect us mentally.

"Once you are no longer mentally affected by a problem, you no longer have it—although nothing external may actually have changed in your life."

When Sutphen asked him how he had done in the group sessions during the five-day seminar, Ben admitted that it had been slow at first. "But the impressions became more real and vivid with each session."

The regressionist-hypnotist decided that since Ben had already been conditioned he would proceed with a session with him, then, if necessary, include another one or two with Wendy.

As it turned out, one regression with Ben was all that was necessary for an understanding of his present-life anxieties about his wife.

During his regression, Ben saw himself as a woman named Ena, working in a bakery shop in England in the mid-1700s. She eventually met and married a young man named Carlton (Wendy), who made his living traveling throughout the country selling various tobaccos for a London importer.

On one occasion, after they had been married for three months, Carlton was badly beaten and robbed while away on business. Two months of convalescence were required before he could return to his work.

A year later, Ena was pregnant, and the marriage was happy.

And then Carlton did not return from a sales trip. The two never saw each other again, and Ena went to her grave uncertain of Carlton's fate.

Dick Sutphen explained to Ben that he was still afraid that if Carlton, who was now Wendy in their present life, went out into the world, she may be hurt or never return.

"You're afraid of losing her once again," he said. "I don't need to elaborate on the obvious, but you must be aware of how effectively this past-life experience has programmed your unconscious mind. You can continue to permit the anxiety from a past life to ruin your present life—or through this new understanding, you can release it and be done with it. If you don't, you will probably carry it forward into your next life."

"Yeah," Ben smiled, slowly nodding his head in agreement. "But you think it's all right to ask Wendy not to take up tobacco selling this time around?"

CHAPTER FIFTEEN

You Can Explore Your Own Past Lives

Psychiatrist Reima Kampman of the University of Oulu in Finland has said that her research demonstrates that people who are able to display multiple personalities or alleged past lives under hypnosis are actually healthier than those who cannot.

According to Dr. Kampman, one of her subjects, a twenty-year-old woman, revealed eight different personalities in progressive chronological order, ranging from a young woman who lived in Russia during the Bolshevik revolution to an eighteenth-century titled English lady to a girl named Bessina who said that she lived in Babylonia. Contrary to what the established psychiatric literature would lead one to believe, Dr. Kampman stated, these were not troubled minds on the verge of fragmentation. Compared with those who could not rise to the hypnotist's challenge, the multiple-personality group had greater stress tolerance, more adaptability, and far less guilt. Internal identity diffusion—a neurotic quality defined as the discrepancy between what one feels about oneself and how one feels that others perceive one—was also greater in the nonresponsive group.

Dr. Kampman suggests that in the ego-threatening situation induced by the hypnotist's request for other personalities, only the healthy can afford to respond creatively: "Creating multiple personalities is evidence of a highly specialized ability of the personality to extricate itself adaptively by a deep regression of the conflict situation created by the hypnotist." [*Human Behavior*, May 1977]

By this point in the book, you may be getting curious as to what benefits you might be able to achieve from a past-life regression. You might want to contact a professional past-lives therapist to guide you through the experience, or you might wish to try a prior-life exploration of your own in the privacy and convenience of your own home.

About twenty years ago—after more than a decade of individual consultations—I devised a number of scenarios for creative visualizations that I can employ successfully with large numbers of participants in awareness seminars. First, I induce a state of relaxation or a light altered state of consciousness in the participants. Next, I guide them through a series of inner journeys that enable them to view important past lives, receive vision teachings, and obtain glimpses of a positive future.

In these states of extended awareness, the participants are able to meet their angelic guide, become One with the Light, and confront their karmic counterpart, that particular past life that is most responsible for what has occurred to them in their present-life experience. I also strive to permit seminar participants to receive a more complete understanding of what their true mission on Earth is to be.

People emerge from these seminar experiences with a much clearer total picture of why they came together with the family, friends, lovers, mates, and associates of their present-life experiences.

Most importantly, in my opinion, they have also been shown that they have within them a multidimensional faculty, a spiritual essence, that has the ability to interact with energies that permeate all life on this planet—and perhaps all life in the universe.

If you use the exercises in this book correctly, you, too, will be able to experience such inner journeys, past-life explorations, and extended awarenesses as those enjoyed by my seminar participants. You will find these exercises especially effective if you share them with another person.

If the procedures are read aloud by you to a friend, spouse, or family member, you may find that you have brought about an altered state of consciousness in that individual. At this point in your explorations it is very important that you do not experiment by asking fanciful or bizarre questions or attempt to become a Svengali to your unsuspecting subject. Follow my procedures exactly, and you will achieve excellent results with no possibility of problems.

Whether you read the exercises aloud to another person or have the exercises read to you— or if you choose to record the procedures in your own voice for your own private exploration—don't give any credence to that old fear about going into a hypnotic trance and sleeping on and on like Rip Van Winkle. If you or any of your subjects should fall into a rather deep altered state while listening to the relaxation process, you will simply awaken within a brief time just as you would from any normal period of sleep.

Until you become adept at these techniques of creative visualization, don't be afraid to use your imagination to "prime the pump" of your unconscious. If, for example, it is suggested that you see a castle or a temple in your mind, you may not instantly receive a clear, independent image. But you know, surely, what a castle or a temple *could* look like, so go ahead and supply a picture from your memory. Once you have your imagined castle or temple in your mind's eye, you will be amazed how quickly some other castle or temple will flood into your mind and take complete charge of your thoughts.

The important thing is that you don't block my suggestions in these exercises or permit your conscious mind to interfere with your creative levels of awareness. So whatever I suggest in these exercises, don't hesitate at first to use your own imagination if the image does not appear at once. In each instance, the essential thing is that you respond to my suggestions and that you do not block the flow of energy for even a second by worrying about what kind of image you should see. Remember that the images that you are supposed to see for your greater awareness will always appear if you keep the energy flowing.

Meeting Your Angelic or Spiritual Guide and Scanning a Past Life

I have always used the device of the angelic or spirit guide in my past-life regressions. In my opinion, such a mechanism allows the subjects to envision a guardian entity that will protect them under the most stressful of circumstances and will not allow them to be tried beyond that which they can endure. The psychological device of the guardian angel has worked for me even when I have dealt with clients who proclaimed their atheism.

In one case a young woman was sent to me by her psychiatrist, who had been unable to place her into a deep enough hypnotic trance to accomplish the type of therapy that his diagnosis deemed was necessary to treat her neuroses effectively. My assignment was to condition her hypnotically and to leave her with the kind of posthypnotic suggestion that would allow him to assume control when she returned to him. And, he added, as long as I was at it, why not try a little of this past-lives therapy that he had been hearing about. Since I was living in Arizona at the time and the psychiatrist had sent his patient to me from his practice in New York, I felt under considerable pressure to get it all right the first time.

But when I explained my process to the hypnotically resistant lady, she protested that she was an atheist and wanted nothing to do with such nonsense as angels.

However, when I told her that it was just fine if she wished to envision her guide or guardian as a glowing ball of light, a "presence," the image of someone whom she respected, or a more aware aspect of herself, she felt much more at ease and willing to continue with our experiment.

I will probably always feel that the envisioned presence of a comforting energy was the device that allowed me to place her into a deep trance, conduct a fascinating and productive past-life regression, and successfully condition her for more extensive therapy with her psychiatrist back in New York.

By the same token, however, if throughout this exercise you wish to visualize *your* guardian angel as a glowing light, a being of pure energy, your uncle Morton, a magnificently winged messenger of God, or your Higher Self, by all means feel free to do so. The desired goal will be achieved regardless of how you visualize your ethereal guide and companion.

I found it interesting to note that in her extensive research project involving 136 experienced past-life therapists, Rabia Clark found that 88 percent of them evoked a Higher Self or inner guides in order to "get a broader perspective in the interlife state." ["Past-Life Therapy Research Project—Part II," *The Journal of Regression Therapy*, Volume VII, Number 1, December 1994]

This exercise contains a complete relaxation technique that may be employed in all of the past-life explorations provided throughout this book. I have used this particular technique with great success for well over thirty years.

You may read this relaxation technique aloud, pausing now and then to permit its energy to permeate your spiritual essence. It is also very effective to have another person read the instructions to you. You might even wish to prerecord your own voice reading this exercise into a cassette so that you may play the tape back and allow you to be your own "therapist" guiding yourself through the process.

Any or all of these methods can be effective. The key to your success will depend upon your willingness to permit such an experience to manifest itself within you.

In this particular relaxation technique, I use the imagery of the ebb and flow of ocean waves to accelerate the process. At the present time there are a number of extremely effective recordings of the rhythm of the ocean, some with soothing musical accompaniment. For maximum results with this exercise, I would suggest that you acquire such a recording to play softly as a complement to the verbal procedure.

The Relaxation Technique:

Imagine that you are lying on a blanket on a beautiful stretch of beach. You are lying in the sun or in the shade, whichever you prefer.

You are completely alone on this beautiful beach, and you know that nothing will disturb you, nothing will distress you.

You are listening to the sounds of Mother Ocean, the rhythmic sound of the waves as they lap against the shore.

You are listening to the same restful lullaby that Mother Ocean has been singing to men and to women for thousands and thousands of years.

And as you listen to the waves, you find that you are relaxing, relaxing.

And as you relax, you know that nothing will disturb you, nothing will distress you, nothing will molest you or bother you in any way. Even now you are becoming aware of a golden light of love, wisdom, and knowledge that is moving over you, protecting you.

You know that you have nothing to fear. Nothing can harm you.

And as you listen to the sound of the ocean waves, you feel all tension leaving your body. The sound of the ocean waves helps you to become more and more relaxed, relaxed.

With every breath you take, you find that you are becoming more relaxed and feeling better in body, mind, and spirit.

You must permit your body to relax so that you may rise to higher states of consciousness.

Your body must relax so that the Real You may rise higher and higher to greater states of awareness.

And now you are feeling a beautiful energy of tranquillity, peace, and love entering your feet—

and you feel every muscle in your feet relaxing, relaxing.

That wonderful energy of tranquillity, peace, and love moves up your legs into your ankles, your calves, your knees, your thighs—and you feel every muscle in your ankles, your calves, your knees, your thighs, relaxing, relaxing.

If you should hear any sound at all—a slamming door, a honking horn, a shouting voice—that sound will *not* disturb you. That sound will *help* you to relax even more. Nothing will disturb you. Nothing will distress you in any way.

And now that beautiful energy of tranquillity, peace, and love is moving up to your hips, your stomach, your back—and you feel every muscle in your hips, your stomach, your back relaxing, relaxing, relaxing.

With every breath that you take, you find that your body is becoming more and more relaxed.

Now the wonderful, soothing energy of tranquillity, peace, and love enters your chest, your shoulders, your arms, even your fingers—and you feel every muscle in your chest, your shoulders, your arms, and your fingers relaxing, relaxing, relaxing.

With every breath you take, you find that you are becoming more and more relaxed. Every part of your physical body is becoming free of tension.

Now the wonderful, soothing energy of tranquillity, peace, and love moves into your neck, your face, the very top of your head—and you feel every muscle in your neck, your face, the very top of your head relaxing, relaxing, relaxing, relaxing.

Your body is now relaxed, but your mind, your soul—your True Self—is very alert, very aware.

Meeting the Angelic Guide

And now a beautiful golden globe of light is moving toward you.

You feel no fear or apprehension, for you *know* that within the golden globe of light is your angel guide, your guardian spirit who has loved you since *before* you became you.

Feel the love as this presence comes closer to you. Feel the vibrations of love moving over you— warm, peaceful, tranquil.

You know that within this golden globe of light is a presence, an entity, who has always loved you.

You have been aware of this loving, guiding, protective presence ever since you were a child, a very small child.

You have been aware that this intelligence has always loved you with divine, heavenly love.

You have always known that this angel guide has loved you unconditionally, with heavenly love, that does not condemn or judge.

Now you feel all of that powerful, wonderful unconditional love moving all around you.

Look! Two eyes are beginning to form in the midst of the golden globe of light. They are the eyes of your angel guide. Feel the love that flows to you from your angel guide.

Now a face is forming. Behold the beautiful, loving countenance of your angel guide. See the smile on the lips of your angel guide.

Now a body is forming. Behold the beauty of form, structure, and stature of your angel guide. *Feel* the love that flows to you from the very presence of your angel guide.

Your angel guide is now stretching forth a loving hand to you. Take that hand in yours. Lift up your hand and accept your angel guide's hand into yours.

Feel the love flowing through you. *Feel* the love as you and your angel guide blend as *one* and flow together.

Now, hand in hand, you feel yourself being lifted higher and higher. Your angel guide is taking you to a higher dimension. Your angel guide is taking you into the Light. And when you become One with the Light, you will be able to move back in time to see another lifetime, a previous life experience that you need to know about for your good and your gaining.

A Past-Lives Scan

When you enter the Light with your angel guide at your side, you will have the ability to scan past lives for times and places that have always attracted you.

You will have the ability to see scenes that you need to know about for your good and your gaining.

You will have the ability to see scenes from the past that have greatly affected your present-life experience.

Now you are entering the Light with your angel guide at your side. You feel the wonderful energy of peace, love, and divine harmony all around you. You know that you and your angel guide are becoming One with the Light . . . *now*!

You are now One with the Light, and you *know* that you have the ability to see and to scan all of time.

You *know* that you have the ability to see periods of time and countries that attract you the most.

You are moving farther . . . and farther back in time.

You are moving back in time in North America. You are seeing this continent when only the Native American lived here. You see scattered villages on riverbanks, tall grasses, buffalo, deer.

You are moving farther back in time. You are now scanning Europe in the Middle Ages. You are seeing those nations that are now Europe when they were only scattered villages on riverbanks, protected by the lord of the castle and his knights.

Now you are seeing ancient Rome, the eternal city. You stand on a street corner and watch the mighty legions returning with yet another victory for Caesar.

As you move farther back in time, you can see ancient Greece . . . Athens . . . Sparta . . . a land of philosopher-kings and poet-warriors.

You move farther back in time . . . Ancient Israel . . . the Temple and wisdom of Solomon . . . the exodus of Moses and the slaves he freed.

Ancient Egypt . . . the Nile . . . pyramids . . . the Sphinx . . . mystery and magic.

Ancient Peru . . . walled cities high in the Andes . . . high priests cloaked in the feathers of many multicolored birds.

Ancient Atlantis . . . a dying empire being swept under the sea . . . its people scattered.

Back and forth in time you go with your angel guide at your side. Back and forth in time . . . back and forth in time.

You see great cities in Africa populated by proud black men and women.

The majesty of Old China, *before* there was the Great Wall.

Wagon trains moving across the western plains.

The French Revolution.

Viking longboats setting forth to scour the shores of Europe.

El Cid standing fast against those who would invade his Spain.

You are One with the Light and you have the ability to see all of time.

Protected by your angel guide, you have the ability to see scenes from past lives.

A wondrous, heavenly light is now illuminating a scene from one of your past-life experiences. You are witnessing yourself in a scene from a lifetime in which you had a deep and meaningful relationship with your parents.

Listen: Your angel guide is telling you the time period . . . the name of the country. You are hearing these things . . . *now!*

A man and a woman are approaching you. Look into their eyes. Feel the love from their eyes.

And now, looking deeply into their eyes, see if you have come together again with that man and that woman in your present-life experience.

For your good and your gaining, see if you have come together again to complete a lesson left unlearned, to finish some work left undone.

Look at the eyes of the woman . . . and you will know.

Look at the eyes of the man . . . and you will know.

They may not have come this time as your parents. In your present life they may have come as friends, teachers, siblings, relatives, business associates, or, perhaps, even as your own children, thus reversing the roles.

Look into their eyes, and you will know. You will know if they have returned to complete a circle of love with you.

And now that wondrous, heavenly light is illuminating a scene from another past life that you need to know about for your good and your gaining. You will now view a scene from a lifetime in which you had to struggle against great odds in order to achieve a meaningful goal.

Everything that you see will be for your good and your gaining.

Nothing will disturb you or distress you, because your angel guide is at your side. You will be able to see everything from a detached and unemotional point of view.

You may now be seeing yourself in a work situation . . . or a political situation. You may even be seeing yourself fighting in a war.

Listen! Your angel guide is telling you the period of time and the name of the country in which your great struggle occurred.

You are now seeing the image of a friend or a loved one who supported you throughout your great struggle in this lifetime.

This is one who was always there, who never failed you. Look deep into the loving eyes of that one who always loved and supported you.

And now, for your good and your gaining, see if that friend or loved one came with you in your present-life experience to complete a lesson left unlearned, to finish work left undone. Look into the eyes . . . and you will know.

Now you are looking into the eyes of one who steadfastly opposed you in that lifetime.

This is one who tried to block everything you attempted. Look into those eyes, deep into those eyes; and for your good and your gaining, see if that one who opposed you came with you in your present-life experience to complete a lesson left unlearned, to finish work left undone. Look into the eyes . . . and you will know.

And now the wondrous, heavenly light is illuminating a scene from a past life in which you had a powerful, beautiful love relationship. Your angel guide is telling you in what country you had this great love and in what time period you had this wonderful relationship.

See now the image of that loved one approach you. Feel the love coming to you from those beautiful eyes.

Feel the eyes of that beloved one upon you once again. This is the one who loved you so deeply, so intensely. This is the one who was always there for you when you needed love and support—when you needed someone to hold you. This is the one who was always there to dry your tears, to hold you close, and to whisper that everything would be all right as long as the two of you were together.

And now look deep into the eyes of that beloved one as you feel once again those loving arms move around you, those lips touch your own.

Look deeply into those eyes, and for your good and your gaining, see if that beloved one has come with you again in your present-life experience—to complete a lesson left unlearned, to finish work left undone.

See if this beloved one has come to you again as someone in your present life—a lover, a spouse, a friend. See if you have come together again to complete a beautiful circle of love.

Look into the eyes . . . and you will know.

And now your angel guide is telling you that it is time for you to return to your present-life experience. You may return with all those memories of past lifetimes that you need to remember for your good and your gaining.

Your angel guide is taking you by the hand and leading you back into the Light of love, wisdom, knowledge, and universal harmony.

It is time for you to return to your present-life experience, but you will know and be aware that the love of your angel guide is with you, guiding and protecting you at all times.

It is time for you to return from the Light, but you know and are aware that your angel guide will always be there to lead you back to explore other past-life memories that you may need to know about for your earthly good and gaining and for your soul's evolution.

You will return from the Light at the count of five. You will return from the Light feeling very, very good in mind, body and spirit. You will return feeling more complete, more refreshed, more attuned than you have ever felt.

One . . . coming awake. Feeling very, very good.

Two . . . coming more awake. Feeling refreshed in mind, body, and spirit.

Three . . . coming more and more awake. Beginning to stretch.

Four . . . coming awake, opening the eyes. Feeling very, very refreshed.

Five . . . wide awake now! Wide awake and feeling wonderful! Wide awake and filled with marvelous memories of love, wisdom, and knowledge.

CHAPTER SIXTEEN

Hearing a 700-Year-Old
Cry for Justice

The young woman from Texas had come to me in
the hope of finding an origin for a series of troubled dreams that she had been having in which
she always saw herself fleeing to caves in a moun-
tainous region. But her regression suddenly took
a very different turn. Sometimes it happens that
way—when it is supposed to.

"Simon," she hissed angrily. "Simon de Montfort, the pig! I hate him! We will never surrender
. . . even if he kills us all!"

I felt a chill run up my spine as I realized that
once again I was meeting a soul who was reliving
a past-life experience as a member of the Albigensian group of the Cathars, a sect of Christianity
that had been branded as heretical by Pope Inno-

cent III. And once again I was hearing echoes of a terrible time of bloodshed, carnage, and persecution as the entity provided me with an eyewitness account of the fall of the city of Beziers in 1209.

Seven hundred years ago, Pope Innocent III appointed Simon de Montfort, an accomplished military leader, to the task of conducting a crusade against fellow Christians, the heretical Albigensians, cultured men and women of what would one day be southern France, who had been declared "enemies of the Church." A true soldier, de Montfort had warmed to the task.

In spite of the young woman's defiant soul-memory challenge to de Montfort that the Cathars would not surrender even if he were to kill them all, sadly, as historical records tell us, he eventually managed to do just that. Although it took him twenty years of warfare against the beleaguered Albigenses, he at last managed to exterminate 100,000 men, women, and children. His Karma caught up with him when he was killed during the siege of Toulouse in 1218.

Over the past thirty years I have met so many individuals with tortured soul memories of that time of infamy that I have begun an extensive file on the "Albigensian Connection." I must also admit that I have a personal interest in these accounts, for ever since my early adolescence I have been strongly drawn to the period of the Middle

Ages that includes the Crusades, the persecution of the Cathars, and the Spanish Inquisition. For whatever it may be worth, numerous past-life readers have seen me as a Spanish knight, and my own inner feelings have always told me that I experienced a past life in Spain.

I get a most peculiar "rush" whenever I pull on my boots or blow out a candle. As weird as it may seem, those two mundane actions will almost always transport some part of me back to a montage of vivid scenes that occur in a blurring mini-second, yet through the years have had a lasting effect on my psyche.

I am walking down a corridor between numerous armed guards beside me and in back of me. I am being escorted to keep a most important appointment behind a massive wooden door that looms before us. The sight of the door fills me with feelings of apprehension, fear, anxiety. And yet I am resolved to face whatever it is that awaits me. I have confidence in my ability to set things straight.

When I have allowed myself to flow into the apparent rush of memory, I feel that I have been falsely accused of heresy. I seem to be a person of some authority and/or high position, and while I am respectful of the seriousness of the charge and the awesome power of the inquisitors who await me behind the massive wooden door, I am also outraged by the accusation and ready to answer my accusers with righteous indignation and an acceptable explanation of my activities.

The sickening cold sweat that comes over me at this point somehow conveys to me images of having been subjected to the horrible ordeal of torture, but my next clear mental picture is that of riding my horse in the Pyrenees Mountains. It would appear that my left leg has been crippled, but somehow I have been pardoned—or escaped— the Inquisition's death sentence.

Yes, as bizarre as that may seem to some readers of this book, all those images come to me in a matter of seconds whenever I pull on my boots or blow out a candle. Admittedly, some times with greater force and clarity than others.

Because I have long since learned that there are no coincidences, it has occurred to me that one reason that so many martyred souls from the massacres at Beziers, Perpignan, Narbonne, and Carcassonne have shown up in past-life regressions that I have conducted may be because "my" Spanish knight joined the Cathars who still fought on in the majestic mountain citadel of Montsegur.

I have continued to amass increasing amounts of evidence that hundreds of those entities who were put to sword and torch during the horror of the crusade against the Cathars are returning in the great spiral of rebirth to bring their consciousness into a time of what we pray will be a greater awareness of a person's freedom of spiritual expression.

According to scholars, the Cathars' or Albigenses' real offense, their "heresy," was their opposition to the sacramental materialism of the Medieval Church. (The group had no fixed, codified religious doctrine, thus were known by various names. Albi was the Languedoc town in which an ecclesiastical church council condemned them as heretics, hence the Albigenses title.) The cultural life of the Albigenses far outshone that of any other locality in the Europe of their day. In manners, morals, and learning, objective historians state that the Albigenses deserved respect to a greater extent than the orthodox bishops and clergy. It is now generally conceded among scholars that the court of Toulouse before the ravages of Simon de Montfort's siege was the center of a higher type of civilization than existed elsewhere in Europe at that time.

Most experts on this historical period agree that the twenty years of warfare against the Albigenses ruined the most civilized nation in thirteenth-century Europe. The pitiless cruelty and brutal licentiousness, which was habitual among the Crusaders, achieved new depths of inhumanity against the Cathars. No man was spared in their wrath. No woman was spared in their rapacious violence. It has been observed that no Roman, Hunnish, Muslim, or Mongol conqueror ever annihilated a Christian community with greater savagery.

Because the testimony of exactly what the Cathars believed was wrung out under extreme torture from those who had survived the massacres and endless sieges, it has been very difficult to gain access to their true belief structure until very recent times. Research now indicates that far from the devil-worshiping monsters that Pope Innocent III decreed warranted extermination, the Albigenses were devout, chaste, tolerant Christian humanists, who loathed the excesses of the Medieval Church. They were metaphysicians, spiritual alchemists, herbalists, healers, and societal helpers—all with a very pragmatic turn of mind.

We may find similar expressions of their belief concepts in the *Gnostic Gospels,* in the Essenic teachings at Qumran, and in the Egyptian Mystery Schools. Most readers with metaphysical interests would probably have felt very much at home in the Albigensian communities in what is now southern France.

Since most of the Albigensian communities were first sacked, then burned, their records and their libraries were destroyed. Perhaps the only accounts of these forgotten people lie in the soul memories of men and women living today. And whether one believes in reincarnation, genetic memory, the Akashic Records, or the collective unconscious, it may be that such an affront to the human spirit can never be obliterated. Fragments of soul may be crying out to remind the world that no orthodoxy can truly destroy the indomitable human spirit or the injustices worked against it.

I was fascinated and gratified to learn that an eminent British psychiatrist had first heard the Cathar's soul-cry for justice in March of 1962 when a patient, whom he refers to as "Mrs. Smith" came to him with memories of a past life as a member of the persecuted Cathars. The research of Dr. Arthur Guirdham, former chief psychiatrist for the British government's National Health Service at Bath, led him to conclude that he, too, had been a member of the religious group. In addition, he came to believe that he lived other previous lifetimes.

In his books, *The Cathars and Reincarnation* and *We Are One Another,* Dr. Guirdham recounts how Mrs. Smith first came to him complaining of violent nightmares. Her distressful night visions were always of her lying on a floor. Then a tall man would enter the room from the outside.

Although she had no precise recollection of what was going to happen to her, the expectation of some approaching event had her terrified.

However, soon after she started coming to Dr. Guirdham, the nightmares stopped. Then she began to tell him her memories of a past life.

At first the psychiatrist was bemused by his patient's alleged recollections of her life as a member of the Cathar religious sect. She told him of her sweetheart in that life, Rogiet, a blue-robed priest. She provided the names of many men and women who had been connected with the group 700 years ago.

As involved as her alleged memories were becoming, Dr. Guirdham remained professionally aloof from the tales until Mrs. Smith stunned him by revealing her conviction that *he* had been Rogiet, her lover, in that long-ago time.

Although he did not openly accept her claims, Dr. Guirdham was intrigued enough to contact a noted French historian, Professor Rene Nelli, and to request that he conduct a special investigation of the historical information that Mrs. Smith was providing from her past-life recollections.

Professor Nelli, a faculty member at Toulouse University and an authority on thirteenth-century French history, first thought the whole bizarre story to be a "lot of noise", but after fifteen years of research, he came to believe in the validity of Mrs. Smith's memories of a Cathar existence. Each time that the British psychiatrist relayed a new bit of information regarding the sect, Professor Nelli's search of the ancient records of the Inquisition produced another matching piece of substantiating evidence.

Clinching the argument for Professor Nelli's

initial skepticism was Mrs. Smith's insistence that the Cathar priests wore dark, navy blue robes. For centuries, scholars had maintained that the "heretics" had worn black robes, but the French historian's diligent research discovered that Mrs. Smith's memories were more accurate than the previous scholastic consensus.

Professor Nelli was also very impressed by the undeniable fact that the data Mrs. Smith provided were not readily available. Descriptions of the Cathars, their character, beliefs, customs, and practices are not to be found in the kind of history book to which one would have access in the typical library. Even scholarly tomes on church history carry scant information about the individual members of the Cathar heresy. The only volumes that could substantiate Mrs. Smith's past-life memories were dusty, ancient records, written in a language that she could neither read nor understand.

As for Dr. Guirdham, he has said that his experience with Mrs. Smith not only convinced him of her past life, but of his own prior existence. He admitted that he eventually came to have an awareness of his life as Rogiet, as well as three other prior-life experiences—one as a servant girl in fourth-century Italy, another as a priest in seventh-century Britain, and a third as a sailor in nineteenth-century France.

Is Rebirth a Deep and Basic Natural Law?

In *Reincarnation: A Study of the Human Soul,* Dr. Jerome Anderson draws an analogy between the universal repetition of rebirth with vegetable life's cyclic laws of regeneration and he terms this process a "deep and basic law."

The delicate and lovely blossom may perish as completely as if it had never existed, but the root rhizome, or bulb, holds in "subjective embrace" the most minute details of that flower. When the subjective cycle, the basic law, is fulfilled, the "subjective entity thrills, expands, clothes itself again with its vestment of cells and reproduces the plant in all its former perfection and beauty."

Thus do the flowers reincarnate and express the same "elemental soul" of the plant.

Dr. Anderson also takes an example from the process of metamorphosis in insects, in which the subjective force is transferred from one organism to another.

If nature has provided for the subjective cycles of flowers by the evolution of the bulb, Dr. Anderson remarks, "how much more reasonable it is that the intense individualization in humans should also be conserved by subjective periods in their life-history. That the conditions limiting human consciousness in each state are different is no argument against these existing. The consciousness of a butterfly differs vastly from that of a caterpillar. . . ."

In Dr. Anderson's opinion, "It logically follows . . . that the individualization, carried to so marked an extent as it is in humans, should be provided with subjective periods in which to assimilate and make its own the experiences of the last physical life."

CHAPTER SEVENTEEN

Her Past-Life Dreams Also Foresaw the Future

When she wrote to me in the spring of 1987, Terralin Carroll said that although she had had a number of unusually vivid dreams as a child, one in particular, when she was ten years old, had stayed in her memory.

"In my dream I saw this ancient stone castle looming above a stretch of flat, sandy beach," she began her fascinating account. "A narrow causeway ribboned across the tidal flat, connecting the castle to the mainland. Three children were playing in the sand—a young girl and two small boys. I knew the tide would soon come in and I was afraid that the children would be caught in the rising surf.

"I joined the children, and I began talking to

them, warning them of the oncoming tide. The children smiled, delighted with me.

"Then their mother appeared and greeted me. I could tell she felt uncomfortable with my presence there. She thanked me for my concern, then nervously ushered the children away."

Terralin said that she might have forgotten the dream except for an incident a year later.

"My mother and I were browsing through a bookstore, and I came across a book with photographs of England. To my surprise, I saw my castle by the sea. It was called Saint Michael's Mount, and it stood at Land's End in southern England. The book described how the tide could come in rapidly and, except for the causeway, leave the castle cut off from the mainland."

Excited, Terralin showed the picture to her mother, then described the dream.

Later, puzzled, she asked her mother how she could have dreamed of a place that she had never before seen. They had never lived near the ocean, and Terralin didn't even know what a tidal flat was before she saw it in the dream.

Terralin's mother admitted that she was at a loss for words, and it would take another twenty years for a possible answer to present itself.

"When I was thirty years old," Terralin continued her story, "I began, night after night, to have dreams of a young man who had joined the U.S.

Army Air Corps at the very beginning of America's involvement in World War Two. This fellow wanted to fly a plane more than anything in the world, and to be trained to be a pilot in the air corps seemed to him a marvelous adventure.

"Then one day he came home and told his mother that he'd been accepted in a new program the army had just initiated. His heart sank when he saw his mother's very visible reaction of fear and dismay."

Terralin awoke, still feeling the young man's puzzlement. He had thought his mother would have been as thrilled and as proud as he was.

Night after night, the strange dreams continued until they formed a complete story of one young man's brief moment of glory in a terrible war that eventually snuffed out his life. Terralin followed the young airman through his training in the States and his being stationed in England, where he began flying missions against Nazi strongholds in Europe. Then, during one fateful mission . . .

He sat in the copilot's seat. Air turbulence from exploding ammunition shook the plane. He had been trained not to move his head, but to look from left to right with his eyes only.

He would glance to the left at his captain— a calm, steady, blue-eyed man—and gain some respite from the mounting fear. Then he would glance to the right and out the cockpit window where he could see the other planes flying in formation, flying in groups of three. He would regain his courage at the sight of them—his bomber group, pressing forward in spite of the heavy hand of death reaching out for them.

They were coming down in a forced landing. The captain cried out for them to get out of the plane as soon as they touched down. The wing tanks were full of gasoline, and they might burst into flame.

They skidded along the ground in an open field in Germany. Somehow they managed to scramble free from the wreckage and run across the fuel-soaked grass.

Then he noticed one crewman was left behind, unconscious, lying in the twisted metal, his neck bent at an unnatural angle. Horrified that the wreckage could go up in flames at any second and the man might be caught in the explosion, he started back for his buddy.

His captain pulled him back, shouting that it looked as though the man was dead and the plane could explode at any second.

Endless minutes later, tears streaming down his face, he started once again toward the wreckage after the captain gave him the go-ahead.

Just as he ran toward the plane and his buddy, a young German boy dressed in uniform came out of nowhere with a lit match meant for the fuel-soaked wreckage. A fellow crewman grabbed the boy in time and held him, kicking and screaming. Another crewman helped the copilot extricate the unconscious airman from the twisted metal. He was not dead, only dazed.

Terralin's nightly dreams continued. With each tortured step, she observed the young airman and the other crew members struggle back toward the French border. The copilot, the focal point of her night visions, still held tightly to the frightened German boy, whom they dared not release for fear he would give away their position.

"The copilot was horrified to think that the boy had attempted to burn him and another man alive."

The American airmen eventually made it to a group of French resistance fighters who managed to get them back to England.

Terralin saw the war progressing until she was back flying missions with the young copilot.

And then their aircraft was once again hit by enemy fire. This time they were coming down over Italy.

His captain assured him that they had crash-landed once before and they had survived. They would do it again.

But this was no open field. This was a bombed-out section of a city.

The right wing of the plane slammed into a low stone wall. The cockpit began coming apart. The scream of tearing metal overwhelmed all other sensations. For a moment he felt that he and the plane were one entity, dying together.

His eyes opened. He felt the motion of an ambulance. He rejoiced, thinking somehow they'd made it back to England.

He felt no pain. He couldn't move, not even his eyes. He couldn't call out to anyone.

Then he realized there was something very wrong in how he lay upon the gurney. He felt a coldness seeping through him, and he knew he was dying.

He felt no fear of death, only a terrible remorse that his life was lost to him—gone before he had really tasted of living.

Then he was alone in total silence and endless darkness.

Knowing that the young copilot, the focal point of her mysterious night visions, had died in Italy after a crash-landing, Terralin said that she could not bear to experience another dream. She knew that there had to be a way to stop these ostensible past-life soul memories from invading her dream machinery while she slept. She decided that she would go to the library to look up books on World War II and prove to herself that such an airplane as the one that she had seen in her dreams had never existed.

She actually knew very little about any types of aircraft, especially planes from the World War II era. Her father had joined the U.S. Army Air Corps in 1944, but he had never been stationed in England. He had remained in the States as a flight instructor, and he had never spoken at any length about any of his career in the army.

The bomber that she had seen in her dreams was quite different from any that she remembered seeing in any motion picture set during that time period.

"It was not large and lumbering like the so-called Flying Fortress, but it was a more compact plane, with graceful lines."

As Terralin looked through books on World War II aircraft in the library, she was surprised to see the exact airplane of her dreams.

It was a light bomber called a Douglas Havoc. They had used the Havoc at the very beginning of the war, before the better known B–17 was put into service. At that time, the bomber groups flew without a fighter escort. Their only protection was to fly in fixed formation and to rely on one another's tail gunners.

The smaller light bombers like the Havoc made their runs so low that if they were hit, the crew couldn't bail out. Their only hope lay in a forced landing. Fortunately, the Havoc was extremely sound aerodynamically and could manage where other planes might fail. I saw a photograph of one with its tail section shot off, and yet the plane was still airborne—a feat that was supposed to be impossible.

Terralin discussed her dreams with an air force officer. "He questioned me concerning the uniforms the men had worn and on various other technical points in my dreams. He was impressed with the historical accuracy of the dreams, but he pointed out one aspect that he considered a fallacy.

"In the dream episode of the forced landing in Germany, the captain had ordered the crew to exit the plane the moment they touched down because the wing tanks were full of gasoline. According to the officer I interviewed, the tanks would only have been half full, as the Havoc would have used up half of its fuel to reach its target."

The officer's point of contention seemed logical to Terralin, but that facet of that particular dream had been so clear to her. She vividly remembered how frightened the copilot and the other crew members had been that the plane would explode upon impact.

As she continued to read about the war, however, she found the answer to the apparent fallacy detected by the air force officer.

"I came across a photograph of a Havoc fitted with a belly tank. They would fly to the target using the fuel in the belly tank and then jettison it before making their bombing run. They would then return to the base in England on their still-full wing tanks."

Terralin continued to be puzzled whenever she reflected on the twenty-year-old year dream that had set all of this mystery into motion.

"Why, when I was ten years old, had I dreamed of Saint Michael's Mount at Land's End? Had the children been fascinated by an American soldier in uniform? Had their mother been made uneasy at the sight of a stranger in uniform talking with her children?"

Why had such dreams haunted her for so many years? Why should she have relived these episodes from the young pilot's life and death during World War II?

Terralin had another dream that was yet to come.

An Eerie Dream of Ghost Planes from the Past—and Future

I stood on tall cliffs overlooking the sea. Planes began flying overhead, old biplanes from

World War I. As the aircraft droned on, I realized that I was seeing all the aircraft that had gone down in that war. I was seeing ghost planes passing across the sky and vanishing off into the distance.

Then a second group of planes appeared—the bombers and fighters of World War II. The heavy roar of their engines reverberated across the sky. They flew by in stately formations—bomber groups, fighter squadrons, all the airplanes that had gone down in World War II. These ghost planes also disappeared into the distance.

The sky darkened, white-topped waves rose and crashed against the cliffs.

A third group of aircraft appeared. Sleek, needle-nosed craft of a kind that I had never seen before screamed across the sky.

In horror I realized what I was seeing: All the aircraft that would go down in *World War III!* The ghost planes of the future!

I fell on my knees and cried out against the ominous sky, "Oh, God, please not again!"

I awoke, trembling in the darkness.

Terralin remembered her final dream of the young copilot of the Havoc and how he had regretted the senseless waste of life that the war had brought.

From what she could ascertain, he would have

died in 1942. She had been born in 1945. From the time that she was a child, she had been concerned with the United Nations and with world peace. As a young woman, she had worked with several organizations, such as the World Future Society, People for Peace, Planetary Citizens, and the Bahai Faith, that were dedicated to promoting understanding among all people.

Was she, Terralin Carroll, a spirit reborn? Had she lived as a young airman who had lost his precious chance at life in a cruel war? Had she in a prior-life experience suffered the horror and misery of war so that now, in her present life she was determined not to let it happen again?

There was yet another mysterious aspect to the dream.

At the moment of his death, the young copilot of the Havoc bomber had felt at one with his aircraft. As a young woman, Terralin had experienced a similar incident concerning an airplane disaster.

She was a college student returning home from class. It was late in the evening when she got on the bus, and as she wearily gazed out of the window, not thinking of anything in particular, a white mist seemed to come up around her and to envelop her.

As if that were not eerie enough, the mist somehow seemed to possess a consciousness.

When the mist cleared, Terralin's own consciousness was flying low over an expanse of water. Far off in the distance, a jet airliner was approaching her.

Then, for a few incredible seconds, she felt as though she had become one with the aircraft.

I walked up the aisle. It was very early in the morning, and some of the passengers had gone back to sleep.

I walked into the cockpit and stood behind the captain. I felt the man's pride in his work.

Then something on the instrument panel caught his eye. He froze in fear, unable to speak. His copilot appeared to be unaware of the problem.

The plane began to shudder uncontrollably.

I could feel the fear of the passengers as they realized that this was not ordinary air turbulence.

The copilot looked helplessly at his captain as the airliner suddenly started down in a power dive. I looked out the cockpit window as the water below seemed to rush up at us. Behind me I heard the passengers screaming their death cries.

Then I was out of the plane some distance away. It hit the water as though slamming into a brick wall and disintegrated.

A presence behind me said sadly, "They're all dead."

The next evening when she was returning home from class, newspaper headlines caught Terralin's attention: JET PLANE CRASHES IN PONTCHARTRAIN LAKE, 87 PEOPLE KILLED.

She rushed home and turned on the news. The airliner had gone down that morning at six o'clock. The cause of the crash was being investigated.

For a fleeting moment she considered calling the airport and telling them of her vision, but she thought better of the idea after a few seconds' reflection on how she would no doubt sound to a hard-nosed aeronautics investigator.

A month later the FAA reported their findings which indicated that the mechanism that was supposed to keep the aircraft's nose level had failed, thus putting the airliner into a power dive. Apparently there was nothing the pilots could have done.

Who or *what* was the consciousness in the white mist that had taken Terralin twelve hours ahead in time to show her the Pontchartrain disaster?

"Was it the spirit of the young copilot of the Havoc? Had his spirit been with me since childhood, impelling me toward a concern for world peace, warning me of the terrible consequences of another war?"

As Terralin reviewed her intense mystical experiences, she could perceive that there were times in the dreams when she seemed to be a participant, others when she felt she was merely an observer.

"Reincarnation had never been a part of my religious beliefs," she said. "Now I felt that I must consider it a possibility. But all I knew for certain was that a message had come to me across time and space—a message from a young man who had lived and died during World War Two."

For Terralin Carroll the message is simple, direct, and meaningful:

"Man must relinquish the mystique of the warrior and the prestige and power of the soldier. For thousands of years men have looked upon the conflict of war as a testing ground, an opportunity to prove themselves. Perhaps at one time when men came face to face on the battlefield, there may have been issues of courage and honor; but since the advent of mechanized warfare in World War One, there has only been the wholesale slaughter of young lives.

"The series of dreams renewed my resolve to work toward what in the Bahai faith is called, the 'Most Great Peace.'"

Envisioning a Past Life as a Member of the Opposite Sex

In order to extend the parameters of your consciousness and sensitivity, try this interesting inner journey.

After making yourself comfortable, relax as completely as possible by using the relaxation process in Chapter Fifteen. Remember to surround yourself with Light and envision your angel guide accompanying you through your memories of a member of the opposite sex in a past-life experience as you answer the following questions:

In what period of time and in what country or place do you live?

Are you male or female?

Concentrate on the body you wore in that past life. Become fully and totally aware of it. What parts of it feel truly different from your present body?

How do you feel about your body in that life?

Describe every aspect of your past-life body. Realize how being a [male or female] made your life very different from what it is now.

How did you feel about being [male or female] in that life?

What is your relationship with your mother?

Do you feel that you are treated differently by your mother because of your gender?

What is your relationships with your father?

Do you feel that you are treated differently by your father because of your gender?

How many brothers or sisters do you have? How do they react to you because of your gender?

What type of work do you do or what kind of training did you receive?

See yourself in a work situation. How do the other workers react to you?

Visualize yourself walking amidst a group of women and women in that lifetime.

How do the men treat you as you pass?

How do the women react to your presence?

Visualize a scene in that lifetime when you are alone with a member of the opposite sex.

How do you feel about being [male or female] in this kind of situation?

Do you ever marry?

If so, reflect on your sex role with your spouse in that time.

Are your life situations as a married person basically happy or unhappy?

How many children do you have?

Examine your performance as [mother or father].

Do you find yourself favoring the child or children of one gender over the other?

How do you die in that time?

What was the most important lesson that you were to receive from that life experience?

Did anyone in your present lifetime come with you from that life experience?

What lesson or work are you to attempt to complete in your present-life existence?

CHAPTER EIGHTEEN

Can We Remember Our Ancestors' Lives?

Harold Gustavson was of sturdy Scandinavian–American stock, and he worked a farm in the heart of rich Iowa cropland. A serious, religious man who was dependable and honest, Harold was strong of body and sound of mind in all ways except one—since earliest childhood he had had a morbid fear of fire. The phobia reached such dramatic proportions that the child would run screaming from the room if Grandpa Olofson should choose to light his pipe at the table after dinner.

Harold's crisis situation was reached when, as a young man of thirty-two, the barn on the family farm caught fire.

Thorston, Harold's sixty-seven-year-old father,

went into the flaming building in an attempt to lead their prize bull to safety. Timbers collapsed, and both Thorston and the animal were trapped in the flames.

As much as Harold wanted to go to his father's rescue, the young farmer was unable to move from the spot where he lay sobbing and vomiting upon the ground. Fortunately, neighbors arrived in time to save Thorston, who was badly burned and required a hospital stay. The bull had to be destroyed.

The psychologist at the local social services center worked with Harold for several sessions, but he remained perplexed because he could find absolutely no precipitating trauma in his childhood that could have accounted for his extreme pyrophobia. When he interviewed Harold's parents, they could only offer their observation that their son "had just been born afraid of fire."

A Fear of Fire Inherited from His Great-Grandfather

This particular case was not resolved with a session of hypnotic regression probing a past-life experience to unearth the source of Harold's phobia. In this case, it was the patient who, after years of mental torment, finally provided the key to solving his own problem.

When Harold arrived for his next session with his therapist, he brought an old leather-bound journal.

"It belonged to my great-grandmother on my mother's side, Inga Larson–Olofson," he told the psychologist. "It is her journal of the trip across the ocean and the story of her early days on the prairie in the new country."

Harold's family maintained close ties with relatives in the "old country," and his mother was still able to speak and to read Norwegian with great fluency. Just the night before, Harold explained, his mother had had an unusual idea occur to her, and she had read aloud a certain section of the journal.

"Great-grandmother Inga writes of a terrible thing that happened to my great-grandfather Nils on the ship coming over," Harold explained to the psychologist. "Inga and Nils were only teenagers, newlyweds, seeking their fortune in the New World. A fire broke out in the ship's galley, and a can of cooking grease exploded. Nils was seated near the galley door at the time; and some of the flaming grease landed on his chest, shoulders, and neck. He suffered very bad burns from the grease, and he became very ill and nearly died before they reached New York for the trip to Iowa. My mother said that although great-grandfather received those burns when he was only nineteen, he bore terrible scars until the day he passed away, fifteen years before I was born."

The very conservative psychologist in the small-town clinic slowly tapped the point of a ballpoint pen on his notepad, not quite understanding what he was to do with this bit of family history. "Are you telling me that you think there may be some connection between your great-grandfather's severe burns during his immigration to America and your fear of fire?"

Harold shrugged his broad shoulders. "Well, you know it's a funny thing, but ever since I was a kid, whenever I would think of fire or I would be frightened when someone started a fire, I would get this image of the sea, of waves rolling up and down around me. I could never make any association before, except, you know, thinking that fire and water were complete opposites.

"Then, last night, when Mom was reading from that old journal, I had this really strange feeling. And while Mom read the story, it was like I could see it all happening, just like I was watching it all on television. Maybe old Nils Olofson passed on his memory of those terrible burns to me. Maybe, somehow, I inherited his fear of fire along with his curly blond hair."

Is it possible that the memory, and thereby the fear, of fire had been transmitted through the genes from Harold's great-grandfather to his own memory bank? Researcher Volney G. Mathison once related a strangely similar case of a fear of fire that appeared to have been transferred to a descendant by genetic memory.

Past Life Regression Banished a Fear of Being Burned

Connie, a Mexican girl who was employed in Mathison's electronic plant, had been doing a clumsy job of soldering joints and wires. Apparently unaware of her shoddy workmanship, she became extremely upset and emotional whenever she was reprimanded by her supervisor.

Mathison was aware that previous analysis had indicated that Connie had an "intense, subconscious terror of getting burned." According to conventional psychoanalytic theory, this meant that she had suffered severe burns in childhood or infancy; but as far as Connie and her family could determine, such an accident had never occurred.

Rather reluctantly, Mathison decided to take it upon himself to attempt to hypnotize his employee and see if he could regress her to some point in time when the origin of the trauma could be determined. He was quite astonished when she began to tell of being en route to the New World on a Spanish sailing vessel.

A fire broke out on the crowded seventeenth-century ship, and in the resulting panic, she had been badly burned.

When Mathison brought Connie back to the present, she exclaimed, "Why should I be so afraid of a little soldering iron after I went through all that?"

It is interesting to note that Connie had a reddish birthmark that covered her back and right shoulder. According to Mathison, this mark began to diminish in size after the catharsis of the hypnotic session.

Healing a Hand That Was Crippled in a Past Life

Back in the 1960s, when past-lives therapy was very new, one of my correspondents, a psychic-sensitive in Ireland, told me of how she had worked with a psychiatrist in Belfast to "cure" a young Jew of a crippled hand.

After obtaining a telepathic mind-linkup with the patient, the psychic determined that the young man's unconscious carried the violent memories of a pogrom in czarist Russia. This particular persecution had included the rape of the patient's female ancestor and the chopping off of the hand of a male ancestor, who had struck back at her attackers.

When the young man was told of the sensitive's

impressions of the origin of his physical debility, he remarked to the doctor that it was as if he had heard it all before long ago. Once the seat of the trauma had been discovered, its therapy could be prescribed by the doctor along the lines of more conventional psychoanalysis.

Can Our Memories Be Inherited?

Can memory be inherited by genetic transmission?

The birth of a redhead in a family of brunettes is quite often the subject for a great deal of rather earthy speculation and teasing—until it is discovered that great-great-grandfather proudly wore a fiery mane and beard.

The unexpected appearance of extraordinary musical talent in a family of folks "who can't carry a tune in a bucket" may well be due to memory-energy patterns transmitted in the genes.

If the miracle of conception, with its pairing of the mother-genes and the father-genes, determine the color of our hair and our eyes, our basic height and weight, our inherent strengths and weaknesses, is it not quite possible, many researchers are asking, that certain dramatic memory patterns may also be inherited?

The Man Who Returned as His Own Grandson

Mrs. Susan George was sorting through her jewelry box one afternoon when her five-year-old son, William, wandered into her bedroom.

Fascinated by his mother's personal treasures, William stood at the side of the bed where she had arranged her earrings, bracelets, necklaces, and pins. Then, spotting a gold watch in the jewelry box, he suddenly reached out for the timepiece.

"William!" she scolded. "Mustn't touch!"

"But it is *mine*!" the boy shouted, defending his snatching of the watch.

"Shush," his mother scowled. "That watch belonged to your grandfather. The same Grandpa William whose name you bear. He asked your daddy to keep the watch for him before he died."

William nodded in agreement. "And that is *my* watch!"

The boy clung stubbornly to the watch, and it took Susan several minutes to persuade him to allow her to replace it in her jewelry box.

That night when she told her husband Reginald about the incident, both of them were disturbed by their son's behavior.

The Georges are Tlingit Indians who live in southeastern Alaska. Like others of their tribe, the Georges believe in reincarnation. Ever since their son was born, he had given evidence of resembling his paternal grandfather William in birthmarks, attitudes, and physical appearance. Although such belief concepts were within the realm of their personal cosmology, Susan and Reginald found that a manifestation of the doctrine of reincarnation in their own home was somewhat disconcerting.

"I Will Come Back as Your Son"

William George I had been a well-known Alaskan fisherman, a healthy, robust man, who had always been extremely active. As he grew older, he began to express certain doubts and uncertainties about the afterlife.

"If there really is anything to this business of rebirth, I will come back to you as your son," William once told his son Reginald while they were fishing.

William also made such statements to his daughter-in-law, and he told Susan that they would be able to recognize him by the fact that he would be reborn with the same birthmarks as the ones that he presently bore. These marks were well-known by William's kin and friends to be two large moles, each about a half-inch in diameter—one on his upper left shoulder, the other on his left forearm.

In the summer of 1949, William gave Reginald his gold watch. "As you well know, this was given to me by your mother. I want you to keep it for me. When I come back as your son, I'll reclaim it—so you take good care of it for me."

Reginald told his father not to continue to dwell on such a morbid subject as his death and rebirth. "You're in great shape. You're only sixty years old. You got a lot of years ahead of you. Keep your watch, Dad."

William was insistent. "I feel that I don't have long too live, Reg. I don't want anything to happen to the watch your mother gave me. Take it. Please. If there's anything to this reincarnation business, I'll be back as your son and I'll get the watch back then."

Susan suggested that Reginald go along with his father's wishes. "Take it. Tell him that I'll put it in my jewelry box. That'll make him feel better."

His Body Was Missing, But Not His Soul

A few weeks later in August the crew of William George's seine boat reported their captain as missing. None of them could say what had happened to their skipper. His body was never recovered, and they could only conclude that he had fallen overboard and had been swept away by the tide.

In May 1950, scarcely nine months after William George's death, Susan went into labor.

As she lay in the delivery room waiting for the anesthetic that would lessen her painful consciousness, Susan had a vision in which she saw the form of her father-in-law standing at her side. The image of the man was so real, and his actions so lifelike and familiar, that she came out of the anesthesia uttering soft cries of confusion. She awoke fully expecting to see William George still standing beside her.

Later, when she held her healthy baby boy and saw that he had a large mole on his left shoulder and another on his left forearm—precisely the same locations as those moles that had been borne by his grandfather—Susan told Reginald that they should name him William George II.

Just Like Grandpa William

As the boy began to grow, his parents found an ever-increasing number of details that tended to justify their decision to name their son after his grandfather. The boy's behavior traits, his likes and dislikes, and his developing skills coincided exactly with those of William George I.

Foremost among the many similarities was the peculiar manner in which the boy walked. William I, when a young man, had injured his right ankle severely while playing basketball, and he had continued to walk with a limp as long as most members of the fishing village could remember. Because of the nature of the injury, he had turned his right foot outward so that he walked with a peculiar gait, which became a recognizable characteristic of the man.

Reginald and Susan were startled when their

young son took his first steps with his right foot turned outward. In spite of their efforts to guide the boy into a proper gait, he persisted in maintaining the peculiar, twisted manner of walking.

For all his bravado and skill aboard his fishing boat, William I was known as a great worrier. His constantly repeated words of cautionary advice to his crew often brought groans of irritation from seasoned fishermen who felt that they were well-experienced in their craft.

The first time that William II was put into a fishing boat, he already knew how to work the nets—and he seemed to know all the best bays for fishing and how to work them.

But he quickly gained the reputation of being fretful and overly cautious. And he seemed to have a morbid fear of the water.

William II always referred to his great-aunt as his *sister*. His uncles and aunts were his *sons* and *daughters*. In gruff tones, he has scolded his sons about their excessive use of alcohol. William II's actual brothers and sisters often called him "grandpa," a title to which he never objected.

Dr. Ian Stevenson investigated the case in 1961, and analysed the data along with forty-three other Tlingit cases in his article, "Cultural Patterns in Cases Suggestive of Reincarnation Among the Tlingit Indians of Southeastern Alaska," (*Journal*, A.S.P.R., Vol. 60, July 1966).

As he grew older, William II was discouraged

from speaking about his former life. Older members of the village warned Susan and Reginald that it could become dangerous for the boy to become more concerned about the past than about the present and the future.

Although he ceased talking excessively about his past life as his own grandfather, William II still persisted in asking for "his" gold watch. "I should have it now that I am older," he argued.

The Man Who Is His Own Uncle

When he died, it was as if he were watching the death scene happening to someone else.

The crowd surrounded him, hurling false accusations at him.

A knife whistled through the air, piercing the back of his skull. He was dead by the time he hit the ground.

Then he could see his body lying there on the ground, blood gushing from the knife wound.

Part of him wanted to return to the wounded body, but he was afraid all the people standing around would just try to kill him again.

Since he was now a spirit, he decided to visit friends and relatives. Then, later, he became distraught when they could not see him or feel his hands when he touched them.

When he arrived at his brother's house, he saw that his sister-in-law was heavy with child. He was overcome with the compulsion to enter her body.

He dwelled there for a few months until it was time for her to deliver. Then he emerged from her womb as Thiang San Kla, his nephew.

And that was the story told by Thiang, who claims to be his uncle Phoh reborn.

Prior to his death, Phoh had been suffering from a suppurating wound on his right big toe. He had also been tattooed on both hands and feet.

When Thiang was born, just three months after Phoh's death in July 1924, his right big toe was slightly deformed; and he had markings on his hands and feet that strongly suggested tattoos. On the left rear surface of his skull was a large birthmark, a capillary naevus, which corresponded exactly to the fatal knife wound that Phoh had received.

It was not until he was about four years old that Thiang began to disclose his inner truth. Although his father lived for only two months after the revelations of reincarnation had begun, it was sufficient time to convince him that his young son was also his brother Phoh.

When Pai, Phoh's wife, heard about the claims of her nephew, she made plans to travel from her home in the village of Ar Vud to Ru Sai, Thiang's home, to hear these things for herself. Although the two villages are but twenty-five kilometers apart, there was relatively little communication between them. In order to test Thiang's allegations, Pai brought a number of articles with her, some of which had belonged to Phoh and others which had not.

After the amenities had been observed, Pai was quite astonished when Thiang/Phoh correctly, and with apparent ease, separated the articles that she had brought with her into two groups—those that had been his and those that he had never before seen.

While this was quite a convincing demonstration of his claims, Pai wanted more proof. Thiang/Phoh readily obliged her by taking her aside and recounting to her some of the more intimate details of their family life together.

Pai was now more than convinced that her nephew Thiang was her husband Phoh reborn.

But the unexpected rebirth had also placed her in a rather awkward situation. Pai was no longer a married woman, because her husband had been killed. Yet how could she consider herself a widow when she was faced with the overwhelming evidence of Phoh's rebirth as Thiang. In her mind and in her heart, Pai could determine only one solution that was totally acceptable to her conscience—she became a Buddhist nun.

An officer of the Municipality Office in Surin, Nai Pramaun served as an interesting witness to the extraordinary case of reincarnation.

Pramaun had been a young Assistant District Officer at the time of Phoh's death, and he had investigated both the cattle thefts in the area as well as Phoh's murder. Because he resided in the region, Pramaun had also heard the claims of the small boy many years later and because of his acquaintance with the family through his investigations of the murder, he arranged to visit Thiang.

The municipal officer was startled when the boy recognized him immediately and even called him by name. During the course of their conversation, Thiang/Phoh recalled for Pramaun the names of all those who were present at the scene of his murder—and he even identified his assassin as the man named Chang.

When he finished his interview, the investigator examined the marks on Thiang's body. The birthmark and other deformities corresponded precisely with those on Phoh.

Pramaun told a Western investigator, Francis Story, that Thiang Phoh's account of the murder was substantially correct, with, however, one contradiction. The entity claimed to have been wrongfully accused of stealing cattle, but the municipal officer stated that Phoh had been a notorious figure in the area, who had definitely engaged in cattle rustling.

A final very convincing piece of evidence of rebirth was revealed when Thiang recognized some land as that which had belonged to him in his life as his uncle Phoh. Nobody had told Thiang of the property, yet he was able to describe exactly the circumstances under which he as Phoh had acquired the land.

East is East and West is West

A point which must be stressed here is that even though the majority of Eastern cultures—Indian, Ceylonese, Burmese—express a belief in reincarnation as a part of their religious faiths, young children are definitely not encouraged to remember past lives. Their mothers do not crouch over their cradles at night and inspire them to recall a prior life. On the contrary, a child who claims such memories will generally be strongly admonished to forget them; and parents will often feel no compunction in administering physical punishment. The newspapers in Bombay or Bangkok do not offer a reward for the year's best case suggestive of reincarnation.

If the child continues in his or her persistence and in the recall of intimate details of another existence, the parents may reluctantly begin to make inquiries about the accuracy of the story their child tells. In many cases, an investigation will not occur until many years after the child has begun to speak of such memories of a past life, which speaks very convincingly against any charge of fraud on the part of the parents. In many of the accounts that have been sent to me for examination and analysis, I have observed that the parents of a child who claims past-life memories have reacted with emotions and attitudes ranging from disinterest to violent anger when their offspring persisted in such statements. All of the parents seemed publicity shy and had no desire to put their child on display for monetary gain.

Something presently beyond the reach of orthodox science or religion is at work here. Whether it be extrasensory perception, possession by a discarnate soul, reincarnation, or genetic memory will be assessed by the individual bias of each reader on his or her own spiritual quest.

Past-Lives Memories May Be All In the Family

Because sex is one of humankind's most basic and powerful drives and is Nature's way of insuring our physical immortality, past-lives researcher Volney G. Mathison discovered a number of cases in which a violent sexual experience left a memory pattern that resulted in problems for future descendants.

In one of his case histories, a married woman found herself in an uncomfortable marital situation in which every conjugal contact with her husband would result in severe genital inflammation.

This condition was extremely painful and would persist for days after sexual intercourse.

While in deep hypnotic trance, the woman told of a past life in which she had been raped repeatedly by a band of sea coast marauders. The terrible experience had left her ancestor with painful injuries.

Mathison stated that on the basis of the woman's genetic memory, he "proceeded precisely as in the case of any severe present-life trauma or injurious situation."

On cellular and bioelectronic levels, elements of hundreds of forgotten or barely remembered ancestors are alive within us. Vast amounts of data are carried in the microscopic storage area of the electrons; and as some researchers suggest, since our electronic patterns transmit detailed information about forebears' physical structures, these patterns may also carry memory data relating to enforced genetic modifications of structure occurring as a consequence of lack of food, injuries in combat, pestilences, and other disasters.

Volney G. Mathison believes that certain repetitive dreams or hypnotically induced regressions of past lives may provide reactivated expressions of harmful events suffered by some remote ancestor whose genes were inherited by the percipient.

Obviously, not everyone walks around bent under with the memories of the trials and tribulations of his or her ancestors; but what researchers such as Mathison are postulating is that some individuals may experience disturbing present-life experiences that contain elements *similar* to the disastrous past events in their genetic line. Such present-life stressful situations thereby trigger images, either symbolic or actual, of those ancient, unknown past events that had decisive effects upon one or more of our ancestors, and hence, inevitably upon us.

"I perceive an Apotheosis of Death," wrote George S. Arundale in his *Nirvana*. "There is no death, only change—and always change with a purpose, change to a greater end. Death is recreation, renewal, the dropping of fetters, the casting aside of a vehicle which has ceased to suffice. Death is, in very truth, a birth into a fuller and larger life—or a dipping down into matter under the law of readjustment. Progress always, and progress toward Unity. We come ever nearer to each other and to the Real through death."

CHAPTER NINETEEN

Soul Memories From Other Worlds and Other Dimensions

Since the late 1960s, I have been distributing various versions of the *Steiger Questionnaire of Paranormal, Mystical, and UFO Experiences*. As of 1995, nearly 30,000 readers of my books, lecture audiences, and seminar participants have received copies of the questionnaire. Of that number, 90 percent claim to have experienced a sense of oneness with the universe. Sixty-seven percent accept reincarnation as a reality and have experienced prior-life memories. Remarkably, 78 percent of our respondents believe that they have lived at least one previous-life experience on another planet or in another dimension.

It was in 1976, during past-lives consultations, that I began to find increasing numbers of men and women, who, during altered-states regressions, appeared to be reliving memories of prior-life experiences on other worlds or in other dimensions. For a time, especially in the period of 1977–80, it seemed as though about one person in five who came to me for a consultation relived an alien lifetime while undergoing regression. In other instances, the people who came to me complained of disturbing dreams or of ostensible memory flashes of life on other planets.

Basically, the subjects with whom I worked fit into one of three general categories of claimed alien memories that I had discovered in earlier research in the late 1960s and early '70s—the "Refugees," the "Utopians," and the "Energy Essences." Rather excited to be receiving corroboration of previous data, I found myself bringing old files out of the cabinets and blending prior information with the new material that I was receiving.

The *Refugee Alien* scenario surfaced from the regressed men and women who appeared to relive past-life memories of having come to Earth after fleeing their native planet because of great civil wars or cataclysmic natural disasters. In some cases, they seemed to recall having come to Earth on a kind of reconnaissance mission and crash-landed here. In either scenario, the aliens ended up trapped on our world, unable to return to their home planet.

The regressed subjects described themselves in their former extraterrestrial lives as being humanlike in appearance, and in many instances the entranced individual seemed to suggest that these marooned aliens were the ancestors of the human species on Earth.

The largest category among my regressed subjects was that of the *Utopians*. The men and women who recalled such alleged alien soul memories appeared to be reliving prior existences as extraterrestrials who were deliberate planetary colonizers. Wherever they traveled in the universe, they erected their space domes in memory of the lifestyle on their world of origin. They described themselves as being dome-skulled, suggested of a highly evolved brain capacity, and they appeared to be similar in all recognizable aspects to *Homo sapiens*.

These alien explorers could also have served as the direct ancestors of many of my subjects. Indeed, many entranced men and women described themselves working on the creation of the human species as a kind of elaborate laboratory research project. I labeled them "Utopians" because their descriptions of their cultural, societal, and political structures seemed so idealistically perfect.

The *Energy Essences* were the strangest of all. After I had placed them in altered states of consciousness, entranced subjects spoke of prior existences as disembodied, fully aware entities of pure energy. In a sense, they were mind-essences that were able to exist on inhospitable, barren planets—or even in space itself.

In my opinion, these entities were not at all to be confused with angelic intelligences. In many instances, the subjects described themselves drifting rather purposely through space. In other instances, they approached specific planets with the intention of inhabiting already existing physical bodies.

I also encountered a number of regressed subjects who appeared to have soul memories of having lived prior existences as reptilian humanoids. They described themselves as being large-skulled, hairless entities with huge, disproportionately oversized eyes, grayish-colored skin, and standing about five feet tall.

As I have indicated, however, I gained the most data about the soul memories of the Utopian extraterrestrials. Again and again I heard of a planet with a reddish sky and two moons. The cities and the individual homes were described as having been constructed of crystal or some material that was crystalline in effect. The buildings appeared translucent for the most part, but I also heard descriptions of the sun reflecting off spires and turrets. I was often told that the cities were shel-tered under protective domes.

The altered-states subjects who recalled prior lives as Utopians expressed a great nostalgia for the culture of their lost planet. The cities seemed to be run according to the ideals of a perfect de-mocracy. Citizens enjoyed total freedom without the harsh by-products of Earth's civilizations—crime, hunger, poverty.

Family units in the manner that we know them did not seem to exist. A kind of communal living seemed to prevail, although each person had his or her individual space and privacy.

Numerous entranced subjects testified that the Utopians ate very sparingly, most often of a con-centrated food that was made into a souplike mix-ture. The culture was completely vegetarian with no flesh foods of any kind being consumed.

My subjects most often remembered themselves as quite short, slender, with big-domed skulls. Al-though they had little body hair and no beards or mustaches, they did often mention longish golden hair and eyelashes. Their skin was most often said to be of golden brown complexion, and their eyes were of a similar golden hue.

While they were under trance, I had several subjects begin to speak in a musical babble of language, which sounded very much like a cross between humming and talking in a singsong ac-cent with a lot of "ls" and "ms" blended harmoniously. The Utopians had names like "Muma," "Lee-la," and "Lu-ah." They spoke often of a place called "Lee-lan."

Music seemed to be an intrinsic element in their culture, and I was frequently told that it was primarily a free-form, nonrepetitive sound that often became a part of their very thoughts.

Soul Memories of Fleeing a Dying Planet

In contrast to the tranquil, gentle lives of the Utopians, the Refugees's altered-states regressions were filled with dramatic accounts of violent civil wars, burning cities, and global holocausts. Many subjects reported soul memories of their having fled the planet before it exploded.

After a time, such accounts of a beleagured, dying planet began to sound so suggestively reminiscent of tales of the legendary Atlantis that I sometimes speculated whether or not that memory of that doomed continent that seemed so indelibly etched into humankind's collective unconscious might not have actually occurred on another planet many light years away in space.

Although the Refugees were generally less able to provide me with the kind of detailed information about their culture that the Utopians had given me, I found a number of these subjects were concerned with the soul memories of antigravity devices, cancer cures, fireproofing formulas, and other advantages of their advanced technology.

Most of their recollections, however, were cluttered with survival thoughts and plans of escape from their doomed world. I did eventually manage to work with a number of subjects who seemed to have shared lives in the priestcraft of a temple on their home planet; but they, too, remembered more of the destruction of the building than their daily rituals or their belief constructs.

Most typical of the Refugee regressions were graphic descriptions of immense portions of their planet being ripped apart by explosions and of large numbers of the population being annihilated. I also recorded several subjects describing fiery crash-landings on Earth or on other planets, as their war-damaged spacecraft failed to negotiate proper landings.

Missionaries to Earth from Outer Space

Sometime in 1980, during my research into past lives and my continued regressions of those subjects reliving alleged extraterrestrial soul memories, I found it appropriate to add a fourth category—the *Missionaries*. These individuals appeared to recall having come to Earth for the express purpose of assuming incarnations on the planet as part of an extended mission of elevating the level of humankind's collective consciousness.

At the same time, in a kind of marvelous synchronicity, I began to receive letters from men and women who spontaneously had been recalling past-life soul memories of having come to Earth as such "missionaries" from outer space.

From a schoolteacher in Colorado, describing a vivid, recurrent dream of what she believed to be a past life recall:

"We are in a rather large, round object that hovers a short distance above Earth. I am being shown a chutelike passageway leading downward, and I am given to understand that I am to go through this chute.

"My feelings about descending are not those of joy, but more like necessity or duty. This all seems to be part of the Plan. My last awareness is of passing downward . . . toward Earth. There is no feeling of threat or danger, merely some sadness at separation from the other beings."

From a secretary in a California school district:

"I remember volunteering to come to Earth on assignment. My role was to be that of one of a group of counselors who would assist the planet to evolve spiritually. On my planet of origin, I was a scientist who worked with channeling light as a source of energy.

"My first lifetime on Earth occurred in the Yucatan, where I was regarded as an oracle."

From a Ph.D. in Educational Psychology in Ontario:

"I understand that this is my first incarnation on Earth and that I volunteered to embark upon a specific mission to help humans to develop the skills to overcome their inability to perceive the greater reality. Such limited perceptions can serve to hinder progress. I always see myself in the past as an ethereal, rather than material, being."

From a social worker in Detroit:

"I lived in a city of light, of crystal buildings, where everything was peace and harmony. I used people's dreams to interpret any forthcoming health problems and to help them better understand themselves. On our world, we had conquered pain and suffering by our mental abilities—and these are gifts that we will one day be able to give to Earthlings."

Researching Claims of Past Lives on Other Planets

The whole matter of otherwise sensible men and women who claim spontaneous alien soul memories or who appear to recall them during altered states of consciousness invites extensive speculation.

Are these people, perhaps because of their higher intelligence and greater sensitivity, rejecting an association with Earth because of all the inadequacies and shortcomings that they daily witness all around them?

Does the mental mechanism of believing oneself to be of alien heritage enable one to deal more objectively with the vast multitude of problems that assail the conscientious and the caring at each dawning of a new day?

The Limitless Reach of the Creator of Souls

While the notion that certain of us walking about on this planet should have experienced previous lives on other worlds may seem absurd to some and blasphemous to others, I have never found the idea of extraterrestrial past lives to be any more difficult to fathom than the suggestion that I might have lived before on Earth.

Nor do I deem it very much more difficult to believe in the wonder of rebirth on this planet or any other than it is to acknowledge the miracle of my birth into my present life on Earth—or the wonder that I was born at all.

If one can accept the concept of the eternality

of the soul and its evolutionary progression, then why should the parameters of Earth offer the only environment wherein a soul may manifest itself?

If one accepts the philosophy of a progression of lifetimes as opportunities for spiritual growth and moral learning, why should souls be confined to the "classrooms" of Earth?

If life of some sort may be found throughout the universe and if intelligent life might be flourishing on millions of planets in hundreds of solar systems, then why wouldn't the Creator dip into such a vast soul pool to experience the awesomeness of the cosmos in a variety of physical expressions?

And if one accepts one God–Intelligence for the universe, why should each soul not experience the handiwork of the Divine wherever it manifests itself?

Journalist Paul Bannister, an old friend of many years standing, became intrigued by my research with men and women who recalled alien memories under altered-states regression or during dreams and visions and [*circa* 1982] set about interviewing certain hypnotherapists and paranormal researchers in an attempt to determine just how common such experiences might be.

Frederick Lenz, former professor of philosophy and author of *Lifetimes: True Accounts of Reincar-*

nation, told Bannister that out of about 1,000 people whom he had regressed at that time, several hundred had described life on other worlds.

Dr. Edith Fiore, a friend and fellow veteran of numerous past-life seminars, admitted to the journalist that she was convinced that some of her patients had lived before as aliens on other planets. What was more, she informed Bannister, she had been able to use certain data provided by such soul memories to cure her subjects of health or other problems.

Dr. Fiore, author of such books as *You Have Been Here Before: A Psychologist Looks at Past Lives* and *The Unquiet Dead,* recounted the case of a nuclear engineer who had great difficulty memorizing things. Under hypnosis, it was revealed that the man had been a spacecraft pilot who had been assigned to transport a group of people from one planet to another. On one particular flight, he had been dismayed to learn, the craft designated for his use was an outdated model. Disgruntled, he flew it anyway, against his better judgment.

Dr. Fiore stated that during his regression, the man explained how he directed the spacecraft by "mental projections." Unfortunately, at a very critical time during the flight, a small child who was emotionally upset came to him from the passenger area. Because he was paying attention to her and was distracted from his flight duties, he forgot vital mental commands. He was forced to crash-land in a desert on Earth; and during a trek to find water, both he and all his passengers died of thirst.

In spite of the tragic ending of the engineer's prior-life experience as an extraterrestrial pilot, Dr. Fiore said that she was able to use that knowledge to "help him remember things again," thus making direct application of past-life therapy.

The clinical psychologist told Bannister that she agreed with my findings, even though she had not yet acquired the data base that I had at that time. She went on to say that a number of her patients had recalled living in enclosed cities on other worlds. They, too, had spoken of domed cities with ramps and space buggies.

Dr. Fiore further stated that she was also familiar with the kind of descriptions that I had amassed of "smooth, golden-skinned people with blond hair who are smaller than we are."

She also said that she had often heard her subjects complain of feeling foreign, alien, here on Earth. "I would not be surprised to find that we have all had lives on other planets," she affirmed.

Dr. R. Leo Sprinkle, an internationally acclaimed authority on past-life regressions and UFO encounters, who at that time was director of counseling services at the University of Wyoming in Laramie, told Bannister that he had found counselees who had spoken of "significant past-life experiences" on other planets.

Readily conceding that it was impossible to prove such past-life soul memories, Dr. Sprinkle acknowledged the possibility that some of his patients may have lived before as extraterrestrials. He also offered another theory: "These memories may have been implanted [by extraterrestrials] in order to program us to prepare for life off this planet."

Most of the people whom he had regressed, Dr. Sprinkle stated, considered themselves to be part of a larger system, part of a larger order.

Dr. Sprinkle estimated that, at the time of the interview, he had regressed about 500 subjects of which a small "but significant" number had reported prior-life experiences on other planets. He, too, had heard subjects tell of the red sky and the two moons. He had also listened to accounts of crystal cities and translucent buildings.

Academically cautious, Dr. Sprinkle was confident enough of his research to tell Bannister that such alien memories fit with the patterns of his patients' present lives: "These recollections are vivid and powerful, and I believe that these people are being sincere when they say these were their past lives. I have one woman patient who feels very angry. She feels she has been trapped here on Earth, and she just wants to get off the planet and return home."

In March 1995, Dr. R. Leo Sprinkle, at my request, provided me with a progress report on his work with alien memories:

Since 1967, I have conducted hypnosis sessions with more than 400 UFO experiencers (UFOers). Since 1961, I have conducted several surveys of the personality characteristics of UFOers with hundreds and hundreds of participants.

Since 1978, my wife Marilyn and I have conducted more than 160 reincarnation workshops with more than 2,100 participants. Recently, I completed a survey of more than 1,000 participants in "life readings," both long distance and sitting sessions.

My tentative conclusions are that many UFOers not only indicate a belief in reincarnation [75 percent of UFOers, compared to 33 percent of non-UFOers], but also view themselves as moving from a rational/empirical model of science to a rational/empirical *and* experiential model of science.

Further, many of these persons think and act as if they are awakening to several perspectives:

A. Mother Earth is sacred.

B. All consciousness is precious.

C. The purpose or mission of UFOers is to assist in the merger of Heaven and Earth. That duty includes coming from the stars to

Earth; living in a human body through many
lifetimes; and now preparing all humankind for
a shift in consciousness from being Planetary
Persons to Cosmic Citizens.

In summary, many UFOers ascribe to the viewpoint: *We* are the "aliens"—to ourselves and to
Earth. When we truly awaken, we shall merge
with others, with Earth, and with the Cosmos.

Reincarnation teacher and author Bettye B.
Binder said that she has done numerous regressions with people who have experienced past lives
on other planets. In her recent book, *Discovering
Your Past Lives and Other Dimensions,* she writes:
"I have no difficulty accepting the idea of Soul
travel from one planet to another, one galaxy to
another, one dimension to another. Exposure to
the meditative state has made it clear to me that
we have barely scratched the surface of our understanding of interdimensional travel or of ourselves as multidimensional beings.
"I have encountered numerous people who in
regression have voiced discomfort with being in a
human body and who have always felt they belonged somewhere else besides the family into
which they were born."

A Clairvoyant Past-Life Reading for a "Stranger to Earth"

Many years ago when she was resting and recuperating at Virginia Beach after a serious illness, Rev. Sherry Hansen, my wife, was asked if she were ecumenically minded enough to have a psychic reading.

"My basic religious fundamentalism caused me to be extremely cautious and doubtful about participating in such a practice as a clairvoyant reading," Sherry recalled not long ago. "But I was assured that the consultations were to be handled as a professional research project and that there would also be a medical doctor in attendance to guide the psychic-sensitive through the process."

Perhaps on one level of her consciousness, Sherry knew that the reading would open a whole new reality for her. She is glad that the reading was tape-recorded, especially in view of the broadened perspective of the universe that she holds today.

Sherry was asked to provide only her name, birthdate, and place of birth. Since she was visiting from Colorado and the psychic was completely unknown to her, Sherry was quite startled when the woman began at once to make numerous references to matters in her personal history that would have been impossible for her to have gained through any normal means of information gathering.

Most astonishing for the research group, however, was the fact that the entranced medium declared Sherry's soul to be "not of this solar system . . . but a stranger here, with purposes half remembered and half forgotten." Months later, Sherry was notified that hers had been the first reading to have come out of that center that had revealed a person who had an origin in another solar system.

Among other comments that were made during the reading that traced the extraterrestrial origin of Sherry's soul:

"We see a time when this soul chose to enter the Earth plane, coming, as we have said, from beyond our solar system, from out of the area of Cassiopeia and into a physical body . . . It is this being's sixth incarnation in the Earth plane. . . ."

"[The purpose for which Sherry's soul came to Earth] is to assist those caught in matter to an orientation with their more Divine Father. She brings with her those outer-space attunements with a peculiar type of technology, a peculiar type of religion, metaphysics, or understanding of the Divine."

*   *   *

"Many things make her still a stranger here, unfamiliar with the physical, unfamiliar with the Earth . . . and feeling a lack of attunement or basic understanding with those around her. . . .

"We perceive from the Akashic Record that it has been the plan of this soul that a cycle of seven incarnations be taken on the Earth plane. And this, being the sixth, we project into the future for a glimpse of what will be the seventh. For this soul has agreed to return for the establishment of the Golden Age, the millennium."

A Dream-Vision of Choosing to Come to Earth on Assignment

One night, thirteen years after Sherry had received the fascinating reading of her previous-life experience as a being from another solar system, we slept in a comfortable cabin near the ocean in Virginia Beach.

Sometime just before dawn, I was awakened from a powerful and extremely vivid dream-vision. In a state of extended awareness, I had seen an entity that I recognized from the Higher Self level as my soul embodied as a male person dressed in the strange attire of some kind of silvery astronaut-type of outfit.

I stood at the door of a compartment aboard what I knew to be a spacecraft and spoke words of farewell to my commander, a woman, who was seated before a large control panel. In my dream-state awareness, I knew that the commander of the space vehicle was a female embodiment of Sherry's soul, even though she appeared much larger and taller than she is in her present-life experience. She had the same reddish-colored hair, though perhaps with a bit more blond.

In my vision, the entity I knew to be Sherry seemed rather upset with me. I sensed that we had been arguing about something.

She frowned at me and said, "*You* don't have to go. Someone else can go down there to help them. It doesn't have to be you."

I felt sorrow. She was obviously much more to me than my commander. I didn't want to leave her, but I was drawn to complete my mission by a sense of duty and responsibility.

"I must go," I said. "Those are our people down there, our own seed."

Commander Sherry sighed deeply, then offered a reluctant smile of acceptance as she said: "Then I guess I'll have to go, too. I can't let you go on the mission alone."

And that was the end of my revelatory dream.

Regardless of how one wishes to interpret my vision—as past-life recall, a symbolic expression of marital love, or a bit of undigested shrimp salad—I shall be forever grateful that Sherry has decided to accompany me on my Earth mission.

CHAPTER TWENTY

Dr. Goldberg's Amazing Search for Grace

One of the best documented cases of reincarnation in recent times had another incarnation of its own when, on May 17, 1994, a CBS television movie "inspired by an actual case history" presented *Search for Grace*, starring Lisa Hartman and Ken Wahl.

As fictionalized for mass consumption, the television drama is a thriller about an attractive young woman named Ivy who becomes ensnared by an overwhelming magnetism for a powerful, suspicious stranger who turns physically abusive. When she seeks psychological therapy for this irrational compulsion and for related nightmares, she is hypnotically regressed.

During the process of regression, she begins to

relive the events leading to the brutal death of a woman, Grace Lovel, which had taken place more than sixty years before. In her waking state, Ivy has never heard of the woman—and she has never been to the city in which her death occurred.

Ivy's confusion and terror mount as she learns that Grace Lovel actually did live and die exactly as she related in hypnotic trance. Even more frightening is the eerie awareness that Grace's murderous boyfriend Jake bears an uncanny resemblance to Ivy's violent new lover, John.

All this is great stuff for an exciting evening in front of the television set, but as renowned hypnotherapist Dr. Bruce Goldberg pointed out, the made-for-television movie made no further mention of the stranger-than-fiction true story of the real Ivy.

"Ivy's past-life regressions revealed an eternal love triangle, a terrifying karmic dance of passion and murder, culminating in the short tragic career of one Grace Doze, a headstrong flapper whose reckless love life ended in murder," Dr. Goldberg states in his book, *The Search for Grace: A Documented Case of Murder and Reincarnation.* Only years later did he discover that Ivy's account of even the smallest details of Grace's life and death could be explicitly documented through contemporary newspapers and police reports.

* * *

In Dr. Goldberg's actual transcript of the regression in which Ivy/Grace recalled the details of the murder that took place on Tuesday night, May 17, 1927, we learn that Grace had ditched her "boring" husband Chester and gone shopping. Although her new bobbed hairstyle, short, sexy skirt, and red shoes might be everything that dull old Chester hated, Jake finds them magnetically appealing. When he picks her up that night, Jake has already had a few too many drinks.

With Ivy/Grace altering her voice to speak both parts, Jake's foul temper is portrayed; and the two of them get into a heated argument as they drive.

Jake: You know what the guys were talking about at the bar? I had to hear about all the men you've slept with. I hear you're still sleeping around.

Grace: That's a lie.

Jake: Look at that outfit you're wearing. I think you look like a cheap tart right now.

Grace: And I think you're drunk. Probably too drunk to show me a good time tonight [mocking laughter].

Without warning, Jake punches her square on her jaw with his right hand. Grace is still conscious, but in pain.

Grace: What are you stopping for, you bastard?

Jake: I'm going to teach you not to laugh at me. I'm going to teach you real good.

Jake beats Grace badly, then strangles her. The next day her body was found in Ellicott Creek.

Dr. Goldberg guided Ivy/Grace to the superconscious mind level and asked her if she knew Jake in her current life as Ivy.

"Yes," Ivy answered without hesitation. "He's John."

Amazingly, Dr. Goldberg had discovered that John/Jake, who had murdered Ivy/Grace in twenty of the forty-six lives that they had uncovered through hypnotic regression, had begun beating her in their present life together.

"There was no way that the CBS movie could reflect the powerful obsession that brought Ivy back to my office to be regressed again and again, *forty-five times,*" Dr. Goldberg said. "Long after both of us felt that our initial therapeutic goals had been achieved, something in Ivy would not let her rest until she had relived the *forty-sixth* life and brought to light the circumstances of what the Buffalo, New York, police still listed as an unsolved homicide over sixty years later."

As a therapist, Dr. Goldberg is not particularly interested in obtaining documentation for his various patients' claims to past lives. Whether or not Grace Doze had actually lived and died in Buffalo was not as important to him as Ivy's well-being in her present-life experience. Ivy was a young woman, who had never been near Buffalo and who had no-friends or relatives living there. Bear that in mind as you read these excerpts from contemporary newspapers.

Buffalo Courier Express, May 19, 1927:

An unusual pair of black patent leather, one-strap oxfords, size four . . . is the means by which authorities hope to identify the body of a handsome bob-haired woman found floating in Ellicott Creek. . . .

The woman had been strangled to death and her body thrown into the creek. Two superficial stab wounds under her chin . . . both indicative of the murderous assault perpetrated on the woman was discovered by Medical Examiner Earl G. Danser when he performed an autopsy. . . .

The autopsy conclusively revealed two important facts. The first was that the woman had been strangled and that she was dead before being thrown in the water. . . .

Buffalo Evening News, May 21:

The possibility that the identity of the beautiful young woman, whose body was found in Ellicott Creek Wednesday, will never be known, was seen by authorities today with the announcement that practically every promising clue has been exhausted without revealing a trace of the girl's identity. . . .

Buffalo Courier Express, June 1:

A small black suitcase owned by *Mrs. Grace Doze* and carried by her the night she was thrown into the Ellicott Creek . . . was located yesterday by . . . head of the homicide squad.

The suitcase . . . has been in the possession of police since last Wednesday, but was not examined until yesterday when *Chester Doze,* husband of the murdered woman, was shown the articles and identified the bag and contents as the property of his wife. . . .

Dr. Goldberg's book contains an astonishing *fifty-four* pages of documentation—death and birth certificates, newspaper accounts, police reports, and so forth—that prove to any reasonable person that Grace Doze, a 1927 victim of murder, most certainly did exist. Exactly *how* Ivy's psyche gained that information will have to be left to each reader to answer to his or her own satisfaction.

"Could it have been the unquiet spirit of the murdered young woman, working through her reincarnation of Ivy, that demanded, at long last, public resolution of the mystery of her death?" Dr. Goldberg asks.

There is one more eerie "coincidence" regarding the case that must be mentioned.

"When *Search for Grace* broadcast the dramatization of her murder on that Tuesday night in

May 1994, it was sixty-seven years *to the hour,* since Grace Doze was killed," Dr. Goldberg said.

Dr. Bruce Goldberg and I first met in person on another May evening, this one in 1987, when we were inducted into the Hypnosis Hall of Fame in Skippack, Pennsylvania. We've kept informal track of each other ever since, and I was pleased to be able to include such dramatic examples of his work in this present book.

Steiger: The documentation for the case of Ivy/ Grace is just astounding. It truly presents a real challenge for the skeptics.

Dr. Goldberg: And the really great thing of it is that it was all done by an independent researcher employed by CBS. This gives the case that much more objective credibility. Since the official records hadn't been searched in over sixty-five years, it was really physically impossible for Ivy to have known about them when she underwent hypnotic regression in my office in Woodland Hills, California.

Steiger: What were some of Ivy's other past lives that you uncovered during other regression sessions?

Dr. Goldberg: Among her other forty-five prior-life experiences were Josephus, a craftsman in ancient Rome; Claude, a fourteenth-century shepherd; Sophia, a Polish pianist; Monique, a prostitute during the French Revolution; and

Doris, a tormented housewife in Philadelphia during the mid-eighteen hundreds.

Steiger: What I also found astonishing about this case is your stating that Ivy had shared twenty other lifetimes with this same violent John/Jake personality. Why so many times together?

Dr. Goldberg: She was caught in the "matriculation syndrome," rather than achieving "graduation." Neither of these two entities got it right in their prior times together. That's why I always say, the karmic buck stops here. Past-life problems simply must be confronted and not be allowed to be carried over. Confrontation is next to godliness.

Steiger: I know that you are a magna cum laude in biology and chemistry, that you are a doctor of dental surgery and hold a master's degree in counseling psychology. Have you always believed in past lives?

Dr. Goldberg: No, I didn't. When I was a sophomore in dental college I was intrigued by the old Bridey Murphy case that received so much attention. In 1974 during my residency, I knew a graduate student in social work who was regressed to nine past lives and who emerged free of two habits and a phobia. When I saw the clinical applications of past-life therapy, I asked myself, "Whoa, what's going on here?" I have now conducted over 30,000 past-life regressions.

Steiger: So as one of today's leading practitioners of your craft if someone were to ask you to name some of the practical applications of hypnotherapy, what would you reply?

Dr. Goldberg: Increased relaxation and the elimination of tension.

Increased and focused concentration.

Improved memory.

Improved reflexes

Increased self-confidence.

Pain control.

Improved sex life.

Increased organization and efficiency.

Increased motivation.

Improved interpersonal relationships.

Slowing down the aging process.

Harmony of the mind, body, spirit.

Elimination of habits, phobias, and other negative tendencies.

Improved psychic awareness—ESP, meditation, astral projection (out-of-body experience), telepathy.

Elimination of the fear of death by viewing one's past and future lives.

CHAPTER TWENTY-ONE

Reborn From the Ashes of the Holocaust

They came to him with terrible memories of concentration camps, gas chambers, barbed wire, swastikas, and black boots.

For these tormented people, the horror of the Holocaust had never diminished. Images of the hellishly inhumane atrocities perpetrated upon the Jews by the cruel and sadistic henchmen of Hitler's Nazi Germany were still vivid in their minds.

But Yonassan Gershom, a neo-Hasidic rabbi who lives in Minnesota, was not hearing these awful memories of persecution and pain from elderly Jewish men and woman who had physically survived the Holocaust and had been left with psychological trauma even after the passing of fifty years. These graphic accounts of the terrors of the Third Reich were being relayed to him by young people, many of them Gentiles, who were being forced to deal with what appeared to be past-life memories of having died as victims of Hitler's "final solution" to the "Jewish problem."

When Rabbi Gershom published his excellent and insightful book, *Beyond the Ashes: Cases of Reincarnation from the Holocaust* in 1992, he told of the time when an attractive, young blond Norwegian-American woman, who had been attending his classes on Jewish mysticism, confessed her dread of hearing or seeing accounts of the Nazis and the Holocaust.

Since neither scourge should have been a problem in her rural hometown, Rabbi Gershom was puzzled. Then he spontaneously entered an altered state of consciousness and almost immediately saw, superimposed over the woman's beautiful face, "another visage, thin and emaciated." At the same time, he could hear the sound of many voices singing an old Hasidic tune.

Although the woman was unaware of what was occurring in the rabbi's inner reality, the effect, for him, was as if they were moving back and forth between two different time periods.

Rabbi Gershom decided to begin humming the tune that he heard in his vision. The woman's eyes grew wide in terror, and she broke down and wept, crying out that she had died in the Holocaust.

The tune that he had heard the faraway voices singing was "*Ani Maamin*," "I Believe," a hymn of faith that had been sung by many thousands of Jews as they were herded to the gas chambers. He had no reason to doubt the blonde from rural America when she swore that she had never before heard the hymn.

At the time that he was writing *Beyond the Ashes*, Rabbi Gershom stated that of the hundreds of people who had told him their dreams, visions, regressions, or intuitions of having died as Jews in the Holocaust, approximately two-thirds had been reborn as non-Jews. This figure, however, is no longer accurate. The rabbi is now quick to emphasize that more recent samplings of such accounts indicate that many more Jews have also experienced such past-life memories.

"Perhaps they have been encouraged by the book to speak out, but I have now met hundreds of people who were Jews during the Holocaust and are Jews once more in this life. My figures need to be revised, for my first sample was limited mostly to Minnesota; and there are fewer Jews in this state compared to others with large urban areas.

"Another important point is that Jews are generally reluctant to speak of their personal spiritual experiences in public," Rabbi Gershom explained.

"You just won't find the kind of testimonials or sharing of inner visions in the Jewish tradition that you will find among Christians or New Age people.

"Now it is not because Jews do not have such experiences, it's just that it is considered egotistical to go around claiming to have visions. There are also the traditional warnings against seeking to represent oneself as a prophet."

I suggested that same reluctance to share personal stories of mystical experience would also account for the surprise so many people express when they learn that there are Jews who do believe in reincarnation and past lives.

"There are many teachings about reincarnation in Jewish mysticism," Rabbi Gershom said. "The Hebrew word for those interested in the subject is *gilgul*, which comes from the same root as the Hebrew word for 'circle' or 'cycle.' So the essence of its meaning is similar to the ideal of the Wheel of Karma."

Rabbi Gershom theorizes that there could be other reasons why more Gentiles than Jews have sought him out to reveal their past-life experiences as victims of the Holocaust.

In his compelling book *Beyond the Ashes*, he writes: "Non-Jews who remember having been Jewish in another life may be disturbed by this fact, feeling that they are somehow 'deserters' from their own people—which, in a sense, they are. On some level, even if it was only through being confused after death and grabbing the first available body, these souls chose not to be Jewish anymore."

He is not suggesting that these souls consciously declared that they wished to be reborn as blond-haired Germans or Scandinavians.

"In some cases they simply wished to be something else besides Jewish, and this desire set the pattern for the next life. After a horrible death at the hands of the Nazis, it probably seemed safer to be born into the dominant culture, without fear of being singled out for persecution."

Rabbi Gershom believes that while there are souls that remain in one ethnic or cultural group for many lifetimes, other souls may prefer wandering from place to place, culture to culture, often changing spiritual paths from one incarnation to the next. For such souls, it would seem that their karmic bond is not to any particular religion or nationality, but to the personal relationships that develop among the souls themselves.

"We can speculate that in God's infinite wisdom, there are many different kinds of situations by which Karma is healed," he observes. "All serve a purpose in the overall evolution of planetary consciousness and spiritual growth."

Although I knew that I was raising a sensitive issue, I had to ask Rabbi Gershom *why*, in his learned opinion, did the Holocaust take place?

His answer was an immediate and forthright, "I don't know." And then, after a moment's reflection, "Somehow it was that something very evil came into the world at that time."

I was fascinated by the belief among Hasidic Jews and some others that Hitler was a reincarnation of Amalek, the grandson of the wicked Esau through his son Eliphaz. The Amalekites were the first to attack Israel on their departure from Egypt.

In the book of Exodus, Moses sends Joshua to do battle with them while he stands on a hill "with the rod of God" in his hand. As long as Moses was able to hold up his hand, the Israelites prevailed, so his brother Aaron and Hur stationed themselves on either side of him to hold his hands steady until sunset and Joshua's triumph. Interestingly, although God declares that he will "utterly put out the remembrance of Amalek from under heaven," he states that there will be war with Amalek "from generation to generation." [Exodus, 17: 8–16]

Rabbi Gershom said that in the Jewish world view Amalek is the nearest figure that Judaism has to the concept of Satan. "The very word 'satan' means 'the opposer' in Hebrew, and Amalek and his karmic group have opposed the Jews many times in history."

*   *   *

As we discussed in Chapter Nine, Edgar Cayce's readings on Atlantis dealt extensively with two principal opposing groups, the "Sons of Belial," the negative, exploitative ones, and the "Sons of the Law of One," the benevolent ones. These two groups seem in many ways to represent the classic dualism of good versus evil. Perhaps the Sons of Belial and the Sons of Amalek are somehow related.

In *Beyond the Ashes,* Rabbi Gershom informs us that the Sons of Belial are to be found in the biblical book of Deuteronomy in connection with idol worshipers.

The Hebrew word for "sons," *b'nai,* can also mean "followers" or "disciples" and, when used in this sense, refers to both males and females collectively. "Belial" is not the proper name of a specific person or idol, but a Hebrew word meaning "worthless." Therefore, the literal meaning of the biblical Hebrew phrase, *b'nai belial,* is "followers of worthlessness." In the two most commonly used Jewish translations, *b'nai belial* is translated as "base fellows" and "scoundrels." —

Regretfully, "followers of worthlessness" can also become very dangerous, as the world was tragically to learn about the followers of Hitler's Nazi party. What might we conjecture about the karmic debt incurred by those "base fellows" and "scoundrels" who goose-stepped across Europe under the banner of the swastika?

I wondered if it were possible that some of the souls of those who were butchered and burned during the Holocaust might be returning because they wish to balance the karmic scales of justice. And could the current rise in violence worldwide be somehow due to past-life Karma from World War II?

Rabbi Gershom explained that one of the reasons why so many people are reluctant to forgive the Nazis is because they fear the world at large might then release those who worked such evil on the world from responsibility for their monstrous deeds. Sadly, one of the more unpleasant lessons of the past has been that politicians and pundits have been notorious for rewriting history to negate the suffering of minority peoples.

However, rather than taking the karmic law into our own hands, Rabbi Gershom counsels, "We should leave the responsibility of judgment to the Heavenly Court and trust that God will, in His own time, call all people to account for their deeds. This does not mean that God is angry and vengeful, but rather that God is indeed the Judge of the universe, who judges justly."

Rabbi Gershom is currently working on a second book entitled *From Ashes to Healing* (A.R.E.

Press, 1996). Although this book will also focus specifically on those individuals who remember a past life from the Holocaust, Rabbi Gershom wishes to include more stories about the physical or spiritual healing that have resulted from the act of recalling a Holocaust lifetime.

"What matters most to me," he said, "is that the stories in the book will be written from the heart and will bring hope to others who are struggling to heal the pain of Holocaust past-life Karma."

CHAPTER TWENTY-TWO

Concepts and Hypotheses of the Rebirth Process

After I had participated in hundreds of individual regressions over a period of many years, I began to formulate what I called my "facet of soul" theory of past lives. Rather than *each* personality going through the process of rebirth again and again in order to learn and to progress on Earth's plane, I speculated that there may be a *soul-in-common* for several physical personalities that would incarnate at different times in the linear flow of history.

Let us say, for example, that you seem to recall a life as a Roman soldier *circa* 100 B.C.; a lifetime as a Persian trader *circa* A.D. 300; a time as a Viking raider *circa* A.D. 1000; an existence as an English crusader A.D. 1100; and a rugged experience as a pioneer woman on the American frontier in 1869. It may be that you did not literally live those former-life experiences as the *same* essential personality being reborn in life after life. During states of heightened awareness and/or such altered states of consciousness as dreams or meditation you may be able to tap into memories that had been absorbed from each of these separate personalities by a *common* soul.

In this theory, the common soul may have materially expressed itself in facets of personality in hundreds of lifetimes and will, therefore, have assimilated the memories from all of those Earth plane manifestations. But physically, each of those personalities, each individual facet of soul, has lived only once.

It may well be that the particular lessons learned by the Persian trader, the Crusader, and the Roman legionnaire have all contributed valuable knowledge to your present-life experience.

It may also be that specific memories from your soul's former expression as a Viking raider are causing certain difficulties in your present life.

And it may also be that your soul-facet's incarnation as a pioneer woman is the one that is most closely connected to your present-life experience in terms of what you are reaping today.

But the present-life *you* were not actually *any* of those individuals in a previous-life experience. You are only able to tune in to certain memory cells of spiritual knowledge in the common soul that you share with those other soul-facets. Properly utilized, an ability to tap into the common soul can aid you in acquiring wisdom and increased spiritual growth in your present lifetime.

Past-lives researcher and regressionist Dick Sutphen, who has always remained open to various theories of reincarnation, once responded to my query about what reincarnation may really be by listing a number of possibilities that may illumine the eternal promise of rebirth:

The Classic Concept

Reincarnation is an evolving process of physical exploration for the perfection of the soul, a system of total justice and balance. We learn needed lessons through Karma (cause and effect) and carry this intuitive knowledge with us through successive incarnations.

Each entity is born into each new Earth life with a level of awareness (vibrational rate) established in his past lives. How the lifetime is lived will dictate whether the rate is raised or lowered.

In the nonphysical realms of the "other side" there are several levels. Each successive level is more desirable, with the top level being the God-level, or Godhead.

It is our vibrational rate that dictates our level after death. The entity, upon crossing over, will seek the level of his own rate, but will be unable to remain in the more intense upper levels.

Due to our desire to perfect our soul, and thus to return to the Godhead, we reincarnate into successive Earth lives in hopes of using our past-life knowledge to live a "good" physical life. In so doing, we will raise our vibrational rate, moving closer to our "soul-goal" of returning to God.

The Oversoul Concept

The very essence of your soul is existing as an "Oversoul" on the other side, possibly on a Godhead level. Physical lifetimes are lived as a form of procreation and expansion of the Oversoul energy.

You are like a cell in the body of your God-level totality—the part and whole at the same time. The Oversoul could conceivably be exploring within billions of potentials at the same time.

To better understand the part-and-whole concept, think of a single cell within your body. Its DNA contains your complete "pattern." If science develops its human cloning abilities to their most dramatic extension, you could be "duplicated" from that single cell.

Projecting the concept from a superconscious level, you have all of the knowledge of your Oversoul, or God totality. That knowledge may be existing within the 95 percent of mind that is not normally used.

Spiritual Lineage Concept

You are who you are. You have never been anyone else, and you will never be anyone else. Yet you carry in your unconscious mind the spiritual essence of others who have lived before you. When you are hypnotically regressed into a previous lifetime, you are actually reliving the life of your "creator."

As an example, in regression you see yourself as an Englishman in 1850. The man actually lived and died in that time period; and after crossing over into the nonphysical realms, he created you as an extension of his own identity in order to further explore Earth incarnation. His "spiritual essence" was introduced into you when you were but a fetus; thus, you are an extension of him.

He is not controlling you—for once anything is created, it is freed. But rather he is feeling and experiencing everything through you. His Karma, good and bad, is your Karma. His soul will continue to evolve, just as discussed in the classic concept, but from this nonphysical, detached perspective. When you cross over to the other side, you will have the same opportunity to experience through others of your own creation.

The Englishman who created you may have fused his essence into several other individual entities at the same time. These other people would be your "counterparts" or "parallel-selves"—which introduces the concept of simultaneous multiple incarnation.

Simultaneous Multiple Incarnations

The frequency of the Earth is accelerating, and as it does, more and more "Old Souls" will cross over as new physical bodies become available.

These souls are very experienced and have the ability to inhabit more than one body at a time. They seek to accelerate the evolutionary process by exploring as many lives as possible within the shortest time frame. It may be that, as the population of the world grows larger, it is actually growing smaller from a "soul count perspective." In other words, there are fewer souls, but as the frequencies continue to intensify, it will be the highly advanced souls who cross over to inhabit ever larger numbers of bodies at the same time.

If this concept is valid, you are only a part of your totality—with all of your "parallel-selves" comprising the whole soul.

Lack of Time Concept

There is no such thing as time, and all of your

lives—past, present, and future—are being lived at the same time. Each historic period exists on the Earth within a different frequency of Time/Space, and thus each is invisible and untouchable to the others. Time would relate only to your perception, or possibly from your birth up until this moment.

If this concept is valid, your past lives are affecting you—but you are also affecting your past lives, as you perceive the past. The same is true, of course, for the future.

This concept can be combined with any of the others that I've mentioned.

The Total Illusion Concept

Life is an illusionary game, created as an evolutionary process for the Soul—or maybe, simply for the fun of it.

You are God. You created the entire environment [world] in order to make the game seem real and to give you limitless possibilities of exploration.

Maybe everybody else actually exists. Or maybe they are only illusions.

In hypnotic trance, the hypnotized subject can often totally relive a past situation. His voice becomes that of a five-year-old child, and he relives a traumatic situation just as realistically as he did the first time at the age of five.

From such a perspective, your life could be a self-created hypnotic-like illusion.

Dick Sutphen has never been dogmatic in his definition of what reincarnation may be, but he remains convinced that regardless of how we may view the question of rebirth philosophically, it would appear that that which we perceive as the past is somehow affecting our present.

And once we have pondered the significance of our past lives, we learn how to transform the present into a meaningful growth experience and in this manner prepare ourselves for as significant a future as possible.

Dr. Ian Stevenson's Research of Cases "Suggestive of Reincarnation"

Dr. Ian Stevenson, chairman of the Department of Neurology and Psychiatry at the School of Medicine of the University of Virginia, has done more to put the study of reincarnation on a scientific basis than any other single individual. His classic work, *Twenty Cases Suggestive of Reincarnation*, which was published by the American Society for Psychical Research in 1966, is an exhaustive exercise in research in which Dr. Stevenson dons the mantle of historian, lawyer, and psychiatrist to gather evidence from as many percipients as possible. Although he concedes that nobody has "as yet thought up a way that reincarnation could be proved in a laboratory test tube," he argues that even in the laboratory the scientist cannot escape from "human testimony of some kind or other."

In his essay, "The Evidence for Survival from Claimed Memories of Former Incarnations," which won the American Society for Psychical Research's 1960 contest in honor of William James, Dr. Stevenson discussed a number of hypotheses that he feels deserve consideration in attempting to comprehend data from cases suggestive of reincarnation. Among these hypnotheses are the following:

Unconscious Fraud. In some cases, other individuals have attributed statements to the subjects that they never made and in this way have permitted the initial story to grow out of proportion. Dr. Stevenson terms this a kind of "collective hallucination" in which further statements are imaginatively attributed to the subjects.

Derivation of the "Memories" Through Normal Means with Subsequent Forgetting of the Source. Dr. Stevenson holds this hypothesis to be most often responsible for the many cases of pseudo-reincarnation. He quotes from the work of E.S. Zolik, who studied the ability of subjects to create fictitious former lives while under hypnosis. These fantasy personalities were the products of bits and pieces of characters in novels, motion pictures, and remembered childhood acquaintances.

Because of the remarkable ability of the human mind to acquire paranormal information and to create fantasy personalities all its own, Dr. Stevenson cites another difficulty in serious research into cases suggestive of reincarnation: "We need to remember that items normally acquired can become mingled with those paranormally derived in the productions of persons apparently remembering past lives."

Racial Memory. Dr. Stevenson, a medical doctor as well as a psychiatrist, is well aware that science has not yet discovered the parameters of genetic transmission. He feels, however, that such a theory applied to the alleged memories of previous lives will encounter serious obstacles.

He concedes that the hypothesis might apply in instances where it can be shown that the percipient of the memories belongs to a genetic line descending from the personality whom he or she claims to be; but in most cases, the separation of time and place makes ". . . impossible any transmission of information from the first to the second person along genetic lines."

Extrasensory Perception of the Items of the Apparent Recollections in the Minds of Living Per-

sons. Dr. Stevenson finds it difficult to accept the theory that an individual gifted with paranormal talents should limit the exercise of such abilities only to communication with the specific living persons who might have relevant bits of information about the deceased personalities from whom the subjects claim to derive their memories.

Retrocognition. Dr. Stevenson is receptive to the notion that the psychic ability known as retrocognition could be responsible for some cases suggestive of reincarnation. The subjects in such cases could be stimulated by being at the scene of historical events, by some object connected with the events themselves or persons who participated in them, or in an altered state of consciousness, such as staring at a crystal ball or in a trance.

Possession. The doctor recognizes the plausibility of the hypothesis of temporary possession as an explanation for some apparent memories of former incarnations. But he makes a very important distinction:

In cases of possession, the entity that has accomplished the transformation of personality usually does so solely for the purpose of communication with its loved ones on the physical plane, and it never claims to be a former incarnation of the subject who has temporarily provided a physical body. In true cases suggestive of reincarnation, there is no other personality claiming to occupy the body of the subject and the entity speaks of a former life, not of communication with surviving loved ones.

The Ethics of Karma

"If you . . . have absorbed the understanding that God is love; that as you sow, so shall you reap; that as you plant, so gather you in; you will know that there is no punishment. You are not punished for the deeds you have committed, either in this life or in the life to come. They are shown to you, clear and defined, and then you are left free to work out the mistakes of the past. As I say, it is not punishment visited upon you; it is but the natural working of God's law; it is but cause and effect in operation. . . ." The spirit teacher is White Lily, through the mediumship of Reverend Margaret L. Fling, White Lily Chapel, Ashley, Ohio.

*   *   *

As I previously detailed in an earlier chapter, the cycle of rebirth and the ethics of Karma are discussed, elevated, and accepted in the ancient texts of most known cultures.

The *Hermes Trismegistus*, which set forth the esoteric doctrines of the ancient Egyptian priesthood, recognized the reincarnation of "impious souls" and the achievement of pious souls when they know God and become "all intelligence." It decrees against transmigration, the belief that the soul of humans may enter into animals. "Divine law preserves the human soul from such infamy," state the Hermetic books.

The *Bhagavad-Gita*, holy text of the Hindus, observes that ". . . as the dweller in the body experiences childhood, youth, old age, so passes he on to another body."

In other passages, the holy book declares:

He who regards himself as a slayer, or he who thinks he is slain, both of them are ignorant. He slays not, nor is he slain.

He is not born, nor does he die; nor having been, ceases he any more to be; unborn, perpetual, eternal and ancient, he is not slain when the body is slaughtered.

As a man, casting off worn-out garments, takes new ones, so the dweller in the body,

casting off worn-out bodies, enters into others
that are new. . . .

For certain is death for the born, and certain
is birth for the dead; therefore, over the inevita-
ble, thou shouldst not grieve.

When the great Jewish leader Josephus learned
that some of his soldiers wished to kill themselves
rather than be captured by the Romans, he admonished them to remember that all pure spirits
who were in conformity with divine dispensation
were able to live on in the lowliest of heavenly
places. And in the course of time, these spirits
would again be sent down to inhabit sinless
bodies. But the souls of those who committed
self-destruction were doomed to a region in the
darkness of the underworld.

In his *Lux Orientalis,* Joseph Glanvil states that
the preexistence of humankind was a philosophy
commonly held by the Jews; and he maintains that
such a theological position is illustrated by the
disciples' ready questioning of Jesus when they
asked: "Master, was it for this man's sin or his
father's that he was born blind?"

If the disciples had not believed that the blind
man had lived another life in which he might have
sinned, Glanvil argues, the question would have
been senseless and impertinent.

When Jesus asked his disciples who the crowds

said that he was, they answered that some said John the Baptist, others Elijah, others Jeremiah or one of the prophets. Again, Glanvil reasons that such a response on the part of the disciples demonstrates their belief in metempsychosis and preexistence.

Origen (A.D. 185 to 254) devoted his life to the preservation of the original gospels. A prolific Christian writer, Origen preached a relationship between faith and knowledge and explained the sinfulness of all men and women by the doctrine of the preexistence of all souls.

"Is it not rational that souls should be introduced into bodies in accordance with their merits and previous deeds, and that those who have used their bodies in doing the utmost possible good should have a right to bodies endowed with qualities superior to the bodies of others?" he asked in *Contra Celsum*.

"The soul, which is immaterial and invisible in its nature, exists in no material place without having a body suited to the nature of that place; accordingly, it at one time puts off one body, which is necessary before, but which is no longer adequate in its changed state, and it exchanges it for a second."

In the *De Principiis*, Origen states that. . .

. . . every soul . . . comes into this world strengthened by the victories or weakened by the defeats of its previous life. Its place in this world as a vessel appointed to honor or dishonor is determined by its previous merits or demerits. Its work in this world determines its place in the world which is to follow this. . . .

I am of the opinion that as the end and consummation of the angels will be in those [ages] which are not seen and are eternal, we must conclude that rational creatures had also a similar beginning . . . And if this is so, then there has been a descent from a higher to a lower condition on the part not only of those souls who have deserved the change . . . but also on that of those who, in order to serve the whole world, were brought down from those higher and invisible spheres to these lower and visible ones. . . .

The hope of freedom is entertained by the whole of creation—of being liberated from the corruption of slavery—when the sons of God, who either fell away or were scattered abroad, shall be gathered into one when they shall have fulfilled their duties in this world.

At the Council of Nicaea in A.D. 325, Origenism was excluded from the doctrines of the Church and fifteen anathemas were proposed against Origen himself. The Origenists, those who favored including the ethics of Karma and the doctrine of preexistence in the official Church teachings, had lost by only one vote. But, as stated by Head and Cranston in *Reincarnation: An East-West Anthology*, ". . . Catholic scholars are beginning to disclaim that the Roman church took any part in the anathemas against Origen . . . However, one disastrous result of the mistake still persists; namely, the exclusion from the Christian creed of the teaching of the preexistence of the soul, and, by implication, reincarnation."

Andre Pezzani takes issue with the Christian doctrine of humankind's original sin in *The Plurality of the Soul's Existence:* "Original sin does not account for the particular fate of individuals, as it is the same for all . . ." But once we accept the theory of preexistence, he holds, ". . . a glorious light is thrown on the dogma of sin, for it becomes the result of personal faults from which the guilty soul must be purified.

"Preexistence, once admitted as regards the past, logically implies a succession of future existences for all souls that have not yet attained to the goal and that have imperfections and defilements from which to be cleansed. In order to enter the circle of happiness and leave the circle of wanderings, one must be pure."

In the opinion of such spiritual theorists as Eva Gore-Booth, the role that Christ assumes in God's Great Plan is that of the wayshower and the intercessor who offers humankind release from the cycle of rebirth, the "circle of wanderings." In this view, the anointed one of Christ Consciousness came to offer eternal life to all people, a "deliverance from reincarnation, from the life and death circle of this earthly living, not from any torments of a bodiless state, but simply from the body of this death."

In *A Psychological and Poetic Approach to the Study of Christ in the Fourth Gospel*, she writes: "The idea of a succession of lives and deaths, following one another, for those who have not yet attained real life—are not yet Sons of God and children of the Resurrection—seems to illuminate, in a curious way, some of Christ's most profound and seemingly paradoxical teachings on the destiny and the hope, the life or death of the human psyche."

"A man has a soul, and it passes from life to life, as a traveler from inn to inn, 'til at length it is ended in heaven," H. Fielding Hall wrote in *The Soul of a People*. "But not 'til he has attained heaven in his heart will he attain heaven in reality."

Paramahansa Yogananda, the founder of Self-Realization Fellowship, once presented three truths to be employed by those who wished to rise above Karma. The first truth, the great Yogi stated, is that when the mind is strong and the heart is pure, we are free. "It is the mind that connects you with pain in the body," he said. "When you think pure thoughts and are mentally strong, you can suffer the painful effects of evil Karma. . . ."

The second truth is that in subconscious sleep, we are free.

Truth number three, he revealed, is when we are in ecstasy, identified with God, we have no Karma. "This is why the saints say, 'Pray unceasingly.' When you continuously pray and meditate, you go into the land of superconsciousness, where no troubles can reach you."

Alexander, the spirit teacher channeled by Ramón Stevens, offers many provocative thoughts concerning the nature of Karma in *Earthly Cycles—Reincarnation, Karma and Consciousness.* Fundamental to understanding Karma, the spirit teacher advises, is the following rule: *Only negativity binds.*

Only acts committed out of disrespect, in which the intent to cause harm is married to action bringing harm, tighten the bond between two persons. Such negativity must be "worked out" through future positive events, if not in this lifetime, then in another . . . Only negativity binds; love and respect *release.*

The point of relationships is not to forge alliances lasting through all eternity, but to serve as foils and feedback for each other's soul journeys. Ultimately, for the reincarnational cycle to be released, all negativity must be worked through and erased. . . .

Alexander goes on to state that an understanding of how Karma is generated and released is essential to grasping the larger process in which each life is embedded.

For it is through relationships with others that you express your soul essence and come to know yourself; relationships are the primary crucible of learning and growth in the Earth system. Karma is the "glue" binding you to others through the long journey toward enlightenment. The goal of earthly life is to grow from the callow, selfish grasping of baby souls to the sublime, unconditional love of old souls. Every exchange you share along the journey holds potential for tightening or loosening the karmic braids bringing you to Earth, either delaying or hastening your release of earthly cycles and ascension to higher realms of experience.

Dr. Gladys McGarey, a medical doctor who employs the concepts of past lives in her practice, spoke eloquently to the question of Karma in the theory of reincarnation:

I believe sincerely that when Jesus said that he came to fulfill the law and not destroy it, he was referring to the law of Karma, the law of cause and effect, which is superseded by the law of Grace.

If we are functioning under the law of Karma, it is as if we are walking away from the Sun and walking into our own shadow—which means we are walking into darkness. But . . . if we turn around and walk toward the Sun, then we are walking toward the Light, and that is great.

Here is an example I use to illustrate how I look at Karma and Grace. Let's say that I have placed the furniture in my living room so that I can walk through it day or night without the lights on and not run into anything. I *know* where all the pieces of furniture are. However, if I move the furniture—or someone else moves the furniture—and I walk through the room with the lights out, I am apt to break a toe or bump my shins or fall over the furniture. That to me is Karma.

The thing that changes Karma and makes it so I will be functioning under the law of Grace is a very simple thing: I just need to flick on the light. In other words, I need to move in the light. When I do that, it doesn't make any difference whether I move the furniture or whether someone else moves the furniture. I can see where it is, and I don't have to fall over it.

So to me, the light of the Sun—whether you spell it *son* or *sun*—is a symbol of moving in the law of Grace. The law of Grace does not take away the karmic pattern, it just makes it so I don't have to hurt myself as I move through the Karma that I have created.

E. D. Walker portrayed the doctrine of reincarnation well when he observed that it unites all the human family into a universal brotherhood and sisterhood.

Reincarnation ". . . promotes the solidarity of humankind by destroying the barriers that conceit and circumstances have raised between individuals, groups, nations, and races."

In the doctrine of reincarnation, "there are no special gifts . . . successes are the laborious result of long merit . . . failures proceed from negligence.

"The upward road to . . . spiritual perfection is always at our feet. . . . The downward way to sensual wreckage is but the other direction of the same way.

"We cannot despise those who are tending down, for who knows but we have journeyed that way ourselves?

"It is impossible for us to scramble up alone, for our destiny is included in that of humanity—and only by helping others along can we ascend ourselves."

Perhaps no one has expressed the ethics of Karma and presented reincarnation as a philosophy of life better than did our late friend Gina Cerminara in her wonderful book, *Many Mansions*. In Chapter XXIV, "A Philosophy to Live By," Dr. Cerminara, a trained psychologist with a specialty in semantics, presented the wisdom that she received from an extensive study of the Edgar Cayce readings while she was residing at Virginia Beach. In outline form, this pattern seems to be as follows:

- God exists.
- Every soul is a portion of God. (You *are* a soul; you inhabit a body.)
- Life is purposeful.
- Life is continuous.
- All human life operates under law. (Karma; reincarnation)
- Love fulfills that law.
- The will of all humans create their destiny.
- The mind of all humans has formative power.

- The answer to all problems is within the Self.

In accordance with the above postulates, humankind is enjoined as follows:

- Realize first your relationship to the Creative Forces of the Universe: God.
- Formulate your ideals and purposes in life.
- Strive to achieve those ideals.
- Be active.
- Be patient.
- Be joyous.
- Leave the results to God.
- Do not seek to evade any problem.
- Be a channel of good to other people.

CHAPTER TWENTY-FOUR

Returning From the Light with Knowledge of Your Past, Present, and Future Lives

To journey successfully on this vision quest into the Light and to return with awareness of your most important past life, your present-life mission, and a significant future life, it is necessary that you place yourself—or your subject—in as deep a level of relaxation as possible by using the process described in Chapter Fifteen. Again I advise you either to enlist the aid of a trusted friend or family member to read the following visualization to you in a deliberate and thoughtful manner, or to prerecord the suggestions yourself on a tape so that you may serve as your own guide.

After you have achieved a deep level of relaxation in yourself or your subject, proceed with the following process.

Your Cosmic Vision Quest into the Light

You see yourself standing or sitting on a peaceful beach at night. You listen to the sound of the ocean waves gently touching the shore.

You look up at the night sky, splashed with a million stars. You can see the sky from horizon to horizon. You feel in harmony with Earth and sky.

As you look up at the stars, you ask yourself deep, meaningful questions:

Why did I come to Earth?

What is my true mission on Earth?

Have I lived before on Earth or on some other world or dimension?

How can I make better sense of my life?

How can I start now to make my future existence happier and more successful?

As you think about these questions or speak them aloud to the stars, you begin to notice a particularly brilliant flashing star high overhead. As you watch it, it seems to be moving toward you.

Now you see that it is not a star at all. It is a beautifully glowing vessel of light.

You feel no fear, only expectation.

You feel secure in the love of the Universe.

You know that your angel guide is near . . . and now you can see clearly that your angel guide is hovering beside the light vehicle.

You feel unconditional love emanate toward you as the light vehicle lowers itself near you. You hear your guide telling you that this special vehicle of light has come to take you to levels of higher awareness.

A door is opening in the side of the light vehicle. You look inside and see that it is lined with plush, soft purple velvet.

You know that the light vehicle is safe. You know that it is comfortable. And you are aware that it glows with the golden light of heavenly protection. You are aware that it vibrates with the light of unconditional love from the very heart of the Universe.

You step inside, settle back against the soft, comfortable cushions. The door closes silently, and you feel the presence of your angel guide with you. You know that you have nothing to fear, and you hear the voice of your angel guide tell you that the light vehicle will now take you to a dimension of Light and Love so that you may achieve higher awareness. You are completely comfortable, completely relaxed, tranquil.

You look out a small window at your side and see that colors seem to be moving around you. Bright, starlike lights are swirling around you.

You feel pure, unconditional love all around you. You are being taken to a dimension of higher consciousness. You are being elevated to a vibration of a finer, more highly realized awareness.

You know that you are safe, and you hear the voice of your angel guide telling you that a loving, benevolent Force is taking you to the timeless realm where visions live. And you hear the voice of your angel guide telling you that you will be safely returned to Earth once you have been to the higher dimension of Light and Love where teaching visions await you.

Colors swirl around you. Brilliant lights move around you.

You are traveling into a higher dimension of Light and Love. You are traveling into the very soul of the Universe. You know that you will receive deeply meaningful visions when you reach the timeless realm where visions live.

The light vehicle comes to a stop.

You look out your window and see that the light vehicle has halted before a huge portal that seems to be composed of brilliant, yet soothing, golden light. This massive portal of light seems to be suspended in space.

Within the very essence of your soul, you hear your angel guide telling you that when you step through the beautiful golden portal, you will enter the higher dimension of Light and Love where teaching visions await you.

Your angel guide tells you that you will have the ability to perceive and to comprehend meaningful visions that have been designed especially to give

you deep and profound insights and understandings.

When you step through the golden portal, you
will enter a dimension that exists on a much
higher vibration than that of Earth, and your soul
essence will be totally attuned to that frequency.
You will have the ability to receive clear and revelatory visions. You will receive the answer to questions that you have asked for so very, very long.

When you step through the portal of golden
light, you will enter a realm where teachings of
higher awareness will be given to you. Unconditional love will permeate your entire soul essence.
Angels, guides, master teachers will interact with
you, share with you, teach you.

And now a panel in the vehicle of light is sliding
back, permitting you to leave its interior, allowing
you to step through the portal of golden light and
to enter the dimension of Light and Love.

You know that you are protected. You know that
you are guided. You know that you are loved.

Step now from the light vehicle and move inside
the portal of golden light.

As you step inside the dimension of Light and
Love, your angel guide tells you that some teachings may be given to you in words, without accompanying vision. These will be insights, thought
forms of encapsuled awareness. Other teachings
may be given to you in visual thought forms, living
diagrams of awareness.

Stars seem to sparkle around you. Multicolored lights seem to move around you. Bright colors swirl around you.

And now, totally protected by the golden light of unconditional love from the very heart of the Universe, you are receiving your first teaching vision.

The first living diagram appears, sent to you by the Source of All That Is. This vision explains to you, *the true nature of the soul and what really happens to the soul after the physical death of the body*.

You see now your true relationship to your soul . . . your soul's relationship to your angel guide . . . your soul's relationship to God, the Source of All That Is . . . your soul's relationship to the Universe.

You see yourself making the physical transition of death in a past-life experience.

You see and truly understand what happens to the soul at the moment of physical death. [Pause here for about two minutes to allow impressions to form.].

Now your second teaching vision is beginning to manifest. The second living diagram explains to you *your most important past life, your Karmic Counterpart*. This is the past-life experience that has been the most influential on your present-life experience.

You now see and understand the importance of this previous-life experience in terms of your soul's evolution to your angel guide and to the Source of All That Is.

You see details that help you to understand better your present-life experience. You see details that help you to see why you are the way you are . . . why things have progressed the way they have progressed.

You see *who* came with you from that life into your present life . . . and you understand *why* they came with you. [Pause here for about two minutes to allow impressions to form.]

Now your third teaching vision is beginning to take form. See before you now, *scenes from future time, how Earth will appear in your next incarnation on the planet.*

You see Earth as it will look if any geographical changes have taken place. You will not be shocked by anything that you may see . . . even if new coastlines have been formed . . . even if new mountain ranges have appeared. You will see and understand.

You are being shown changes in society . . . art . . . politics . . . economics . . . clothing styles.

You are being shown the skylines of cities. You will not be shocked by anything that you may see

. . . even if cities are underground . . . even if they are domed and encased . . . even if they are destroyed. You will see and understand.

As you gaze into the future, you have the ability to see an important future-life experience of your soul that you will live on Earth . . . or elsewhere.

See yourself . . . the color of your hair and eyes . . . whether you are male . . . female . . . or androgynous. See what kind of clothing are are wearing.

See your environment. Your domestic life-support systems.

See *who* has come with you from your present-life experience or from any other previous-life experience. See and understand *why* they have come with you. [Pause here for about two minutes to allow impressions to form.]

And now your fourth living diagram appears. You will now receive insights as to *your true mission on Earth . . . why your soul came to this planet in the first place*.

You see and understand *why* and *when* you first chose to put on the fleshly clothes of Earth.

You see *why* and *when* you first chose to submit to the karmic laws that bind this planet.

You see and understand *what it is that you are to accomplish in your soul's evolution in Earth's place of learning*. [Pause here for about two minutes to allow impressions to form.]

*　　*　　*

And now your angel guide is leading you back through the portal of golden light. It is time for you to return from the dimension of Light and Love.

The vehicle of light awaits to take you back to Earth time, back to human time, back to present time, back to your present-life experience.

You enter the vehicle of light, and the panel slides closed behind you. Colors and lights begin to swirl around you.

As you return from the dimension of Light and Love, your angel guide tells you that you will remember all that you need to know for your good and your gaining.

You will be strengthened to face the challenges and the learning experiences of your life on the Earth plane.

You are now awakening . . . surrounded by light and by pure, unconditional love.

You feel very, very good in mind, body, and spirit. You feel better than you have felt in weeks . . . months . . . years.

You will awaken fully at the count of five.

We Are So Much More than "Mere Humans"—We Are Eternal Souls

Not long before his own passing, I asked the famed British seer John Pendragon why he thought it was that in spite of the assurances of mystics and religionists of the survival of the soul, the great majority of people remained afraid of death.

"If we reincarnate, as I believe we do," he replied, "we may receive a glimpse beforehand of what will happen to us in our coming Earth life. We may see what suffering lies ahead of us in the body's rebirth.

"When we enter death, nature may draw down the blind, so to speak, and we may have difficulty recalling the happy things we have experienced in the interim of waiting or perhaps during the last time we had a physical body.

"Furthermore, nature has given us the law of self-preservation. If we did not have the fear of death to encourage us to preserve ourselves, we should allow our physical bodies to be destroyed before it was our time. It is the fear of death that keeps us locked tightly in our physical bodies until such time as we have learned the lessons of life and worked off some of our Karma."

Becoming philosophical about the twists and turns of his Earth-walk, Pendragon wrote the following:

And so, as Pepys would have said, my story ends. It has been a rough road and a long one. In some instances, I doubtless acted foolishly and possibly, to use a rather crude expression, 'spat in my own eye.' But looking back on the trail, I see that fate played a big part . . . This causes me to meditate upon Carlyle who, in his old age, was found sitting nude after a bath, his gnarled hands clutching his body here and there. "What am I? What am I? What am I?" he kept muttering. What, indeed, is man?

Where is the ego?

Am I the emaciated baby in the arms of poor old Lizzie? Am I that little golden-headed boy sitting up in Great-Aunt Jane's four-poster, saying, "Listen to the fiddlers?" Or am I that lad in motley clothing imitating Charlie Chaplin with Grandad Hazel? Am I the boy who made that poignant and mysterious trip to the cemetery, all alone but for his dog? Am I the youth who made love to a dark-haired girl among her father's coffins? Or am I the young man who took those long cycle rides through London to sit at the bedside of the woman he loved? Am I that hoarse-voiced pseudo-Cockney yelling in the markets of the city, "Anybody want to buy a fountain pen for a bob?"

It would seem to me that life has no end, no beginning, but that underneath are the everlasting arms.

A few miles away from my present home stands the ancestral castle of Anne Boleyn, where Henry VIII came to court her. I trust that the phantom of the luckless Anne will not haunt me if

I make so bold as to use her family motto, for more than most it seems to fit my life: *"Post tenebris, spero lucem."* "After the darkness, my hope is in the dawn."

Paramahansa Yogananda, author of *Autobiography of a Yogi,* reminds us that for a few incarnations we may have been human beings, but throughout eternity, we have been God's children. "Never think of yourself as a sinner, because sin and ignorance are only mortal nightmares," he said. "When we will awaken in God, we will find that we—the soul, the pure consciousness—never did anything wrong. Untainted by mortal experiences, we are and ever have been the [children] of God."

The great Yogi goes on to say that we should never allow ourselves to be limited to the consciousness that we are male or female: "You are a soul made in God's image. . . . The wisest course is to remember always, 'I am neither man nor woman; I am Spirit.' Then you will rid yourself of the limiting consciousness of both tendencies; you will realize your highest potential, whether you are incarnate as a man or a woman."

What does it mean to be human?

The psalmist assessed that ever-provocative question and decided that to be human was to be a little lower than the angels.

Shakespeare marveled at what a splendid piece of work a human being was: "How noble in reason! How infinite in faculty! In form and moving, how express and admirable! In action, how like an angel! In apprehension, how like a god!"

Now, granted, we may not all appear quite so splendid at any given moment. It is sometimes very difficult to be noble, admirable, angelic, and godlike seven days a week. The mortgage is due; Billy needs braces on his teeth; the car won't start; and the new shoes that were on sale are too tight. On those days, we feel mean, nasty, and irritable—and no psalmist or poet can make us see the god-spark within.

The French philosopher Pascal once gave expression to the often contradictory nature of humankind. "What a confused chaos! What a subject of contradiction! A professed judge of all things, and yet a feeble worm of the earth! The great depository and guardian of truth, and yet a mere huddle of uncertainty! The glory and scandal of the universe!"

Some days when we open the morning newspaper, listen to the news on the car radio, and view the evening television newscasts, there certainly seems to be a whole lot more scandal than glory going on.

While we may look around us and readily perceive acts of violence, degradation, obscenity, and awful destruction, I believe that humankind most certainly has the choice to become more than conditioned-reflex products of its many planetary environments. It may, however, take a lot of education, understanding, love, and time for the majority of us to apprehend that such a choice truly exists.

Indeed, it may take many years, even generations, before the greater portion of humankind deduces that they truly are more than a chance arrangement of biochemical compounds.

It may require several lifetimes in the Great Cosmic Circle of Death and Rebirth before enlightened members of the great masses of humanity elect to become the sons and daughters of the Divine, rather than the cousins of laboratory guinea pigs.

Still more lifetimes of transformed humanhood may have to evolve through the universal cycles of death and resurrection before all men and women know that they need not be trapped in the same cycles that imprison the atoms of hydrogen and oxygen.

And it may well be the inherent ability of the individual Higher Self to explore soul memories of past lives that will one day grant humankind a new golden age, a recognition of our cosmic heritage, and the final and ultimate answer to the age-old troublesome question: "What does it mean to be human?"

REFERENCES AND RESOURCES

Chapter Two: Using Past-Life Memories to Solve Present-Life Problems

Richard Sutphen's classic *You Were Born Again to Be Together* (Pocket Books, 1976) has remained in print since publication. Other works include *Past Lives, Future Loves, Predestined Love,* and *Earthly Purpose.* His wife, Tara, has authored *Blame It On Your Past Lives* and conducts workshops and seminars with Richard. A combination catalog/magazine is sent free to those who attend a Sutphen seminar or who have purchased Valley of the Sun products. Write to Valley of the Sun Publishing, Box 38, Malibu, California 90265.

Benjamin Smith is available for regressions, workshops, and seminars. Write to him at 2929 SE Mile Hill Drive, Suite A–6, Port Orchard, Washington 98366–6201.

Chapter Three: We are Souls that Choose Human Bodies

Bettye B. Binder is president of the Association for Past-Life Research and Therapies. She has conducted over 3,400 past-life regressions with individuals and has taught over 15,000 in workshops and classes since 1980. Her six published works include *Past Life Regression Guidebook* and *Past Lives, Present Karma Workbook*. Her most recent book is *Discovering Your Past Lives and Other Dimensions*. She is the owner of Reincarnation Books/Tapes, PO Box 7781, Culver City, California 90233–7781.

The account of Alicia Caldwell has been adapted from a longer version that appeared in *True Psychic Inquirer,* Spring 1987.

F. R. "Nick" Nocerino is a well-known teacher of metaphysics and a psychical researcher. His address is PO Box 302, Pinole, California 94564.

Chapter Five: Will the Real Mark Twain Please Stand Up?

Recommended reading:
Bernstein, Morey. *The Search for Bridey Murphy*. New York: Doubleday, 1956. This is the book that, in a large sense, truly set the concept of past-lives regression in motion, at least in the United States. Contrary to popular academic pronouncements, the Bridey Murphy case was not "exposed" as a fraud. The serious student of past-lives research should be familiar with its contents.

Grant, Joan. *Far Memory*. New York: Avon, 1969.

Montgomery, Ruth. *Here and Hereafter*. New York: Coward-McCann, 1968.

Chapter Six: Researching Impossible Memories

The complete story of Jonathan Powell is told by Loring G. Williams and Brad Steiger in *Other Lives*, New York: Hawthorn, 1969.

Chapter Eight: The Higher Self Healing of Helen

Russell C. Davis, Ph.D., is a past-lives therapist with many years of experience. He is editor of *The Journal of Regression Therapy*, which is published by the Association for Past-Life Research and Therapies, Inc., a nonprofit organization, P.O Box 20151, Riverside, California. Contact Dr. Russell C. Davis at 3005 Fourth Avenue, Marion, Iowa 50302.

Chapter Nine: The United States of Atlantis

The Association for Research and Enlightenment (ARE) is located at Atlantic Avenue and 67th Street, PO Box 595, Virginia Beach, Virginia 23451.

Recommended reading:

Cayce, Edgar Evans. *Edgar Cayce on Atlantis*. New York: Paperback Library, 1968.

Langley, Noel. *Edgar Cayce on Reincarnation*. New York: Paperback Library, 1967.

Stearn, Jess. *The Sleeping Prophet*. New York: Bantam, 1967.

Chapter Ten: Atlantis's Temple Beautiful Rises Again in Phoenix

ARE Clinic, 4018 N. 40th Street, Phoenix, Arizona 85018.

Stella: One Woman's Victory Over Cancer, by Stella Andres with Brad Steiger, may be obtained from Synergy Books, 2017 Ventura Drive, Tempe, Arizona 85282.

Chapter Eleven: Viewing Reincarnation through the Mystic Mind

Recommended reading:
Roberts, Jane: *The Seth Material.* Englewood Cliffs, New Jersey: Prentice–Hall, 1970.

Steiger, Brad: *The Psychic Feats of Olof Jonsson.* Englewood Cliffs, New Jersey: Prentice–Hall, 1971.

Patricia–Rochelle Diegel may be contacted at 1716 Sombrero Drive, Las Vegas, Nevada 89109–2565.

John Harricharan gives highly spiritual past-life readings: 2130 Mark Hall Court, Marietta, Georgia 30062.

Lois East combines past-life readings with a portrait of the subject's incarnation(s): P.O. Box 280843, Lakewood, Colorado 80228.

Chapter Thirteen: Past-Lives Therapy Heals a Volatile Relationship

Shala Mattingly, 330 W. 58th Street, Suite 8–P, New York, NY 10019.

Chapter Sixteen: Hearing a 700-Year-Old Cry for Justice

Recommended reading:

Guirdham, Arthur. *We Are One Another*. Wellingborough, Northamptonshire: Turnstone Press Limited, 1974.

————. *The Cathars and Reincarnation*. Wellingborough, Northamptonshire: Turnstone Press Limited, 1972.

Chapter Seventeen: Her Past-Life Dreams Also Saw the Future

Terralin Carroll's story appeared in a different version in *True Psychic Inquirer*, Summer, 1987.

Chapter Nineteen: Soul Memories from Other Worlds and Other Dimensions

Dr. R. Leo Sprinkle may be contacted at 406½ S. 21 Street, Laramie, Wyoming 82070.

Dr. Edith Fiore, 20688 Fourth Street, Saratoga, California 95070.

Chapter Twenty: Dr. Goldberg's Amazing Search for Grace

Dr. Bruce Goldberg is the author of the breakthrough book, *Past Lives-Future Lives,* as well as *The Search for Grace.* He gives lectures and seminars on hypnosis and regression and progression therapy as well. He is also a consultant to corporations, attorneys, and local and network media. For information on self-hypnosis tapes, speaking engagements, or private sessions, contact him directly by writing to: Bruce Goldberg, DDS, M.S., 4300 Natoma Avenue, Woodland Hills, California 91365.

Chapter Twenty-One: Reborn from the Ashes of the Holocaust

Rabbi Yonassan Gershom's *Beyond the Ashes* is published by the A.R.E. Press, 68 and Atlantic Avenue, P.O. Box 656, Virginia Beach, Virginia 23451–0656. Rabbi Gershom may be contacted by writing to P. O. Box 555, Sandstone, Minnesota 55072–0555. Please include a stamped, self-addressed envelope.

Chapter Twenty-Two: Concepts and Hypotheses of the Rebirth Process

Recommended reading:
Ebon, Martin (ed.). *Reincarnation in the Twentieth Century.* New York: Signet, 1970.
Stearn, Jess. *Yoga, Youth and Reincarnation.* New York: Doubleday, 1965.
Stevenson, Ian. *Twenty Cases Suggestive of Reincarnation.* New York: American Society for Psychical Research, 1966.

Chapter Twenty-Three: The Ethics of Karma

Earthly Cycles: Reincarnation, Karma and Consciousness is published by Pepperwood Press, PO Box 422H, Ojai, California 93024. You may write for a free brochure of Alexander's books, tapes, and newsletter.

Recommended reading:
Cerminara, Gina. *Many Mansions.* New York: William Morrow, 1950.
———. *Many Lives, Many Loves.* New York: William Sloane Associates, 1963.
Head, Joseph and Cranston, S. L. (ed.) *Reincarna-*

tion: An East-West Anthology. Wheaton, Illinois: Quest, 1968.

Lafferty, LaVedi and Hollowell, Bud. *The Eternal Dance*. St. Paul: Llewellyn, 1985.

Chapter Twenty-Four: Returning from the Light with Knowledge of Your Past, Present, and Future Lives

If you would like to obtain a copy of the *Steiger Questionnaire of Mystical, Paranormal, and UFO Experiences*, plus a listing of Sherry and Brad Steiger's books and awareness tapes, please send a stamped, self-addressed #10 envelope to Timewalker Productions, PO Box 434, Forest City, Iowa 50436.